Life Lessons from Veterans

Also by Rick Tocquigny

Life Lessons from Family Vacations
Life Lessons for Graduates: All Ages & Stages

Life Lessons from Veterans

Rick Tocquigny

TAYLOR TRADE PUBLISHING
Lanham • Boulder • New York • London

Published by Taylor Trade Publishing
An imprint of The Rowman & Littlefield Publishing Group, Inc.
4501 Forbes Boulevard, Suite 200, Lanham, Maryland 20706
www.rowman.com

Unit A, Whitacre Mews, 26-34 Stannary Street, London SE11 4AB

Distributed by NATIONAL BOOK NETWORK

British Library Cataloguing in Publication Information Available

Library of Congress Cataloging-in-Publication Data

Tocquigny, Rick, 1955–
  Life lessons from veterans / Rick Tocquigny.
     pages cm
  Includes bibliographical references.
  ISBN 978-1-63076-135-6 (hardcover) — ISBN 978-1-63076-136-3 (e-book)
  1. Veterans—United States—Biography. 2. Soldiers—United States—Biography.
  3. United States—Armed Forces—Biography. 4. World War, 1939–1945—United
  States—Biography. 5. United States—History, Military—20th century—Biography.
  6. United States—History, Military—21st century—Biography. 7. Conduct of life.
  I. Title.
  U52.T64 2016
  355.0092'273—dc23
                                                                  2015031407

♾™ The paper used in this publication meets the minimum requirements of
American National Standard for Information Sciences—Permanence of Paper
for Printed Library Materials, ANSI/NISO Z39.48-1992.

Printed in the United States of America

This book is dedicated to the men and women who have served in the United States Military.

For those who have fallen: Fathers and Mothers, Brothers and Sisters, Sons and Daughters . . . all answering the Call.

You sacrificed your time, service, and in many cases, your ultimate life in defense of America's freedom. We reflect deeply on what your lives might have been and honor your service by retelling your life lessons. Like every soldier that ever served, each lesson is uniquely different and often profound. Our deepest regret is that many stories have eluded us, especially inside our own family.

Take up the challenge from the Veterans History Project to capture your loved ones' story . . . so that history may enlighten future generations.

Contents

HEROICS

IN THE TRENCHES

AFTER THE BATTLE

~

Acknowledgments

And without you . . .

*First and foremost, I am thankful for the Veterans who have served
America. Their stories represent rare lessons of bravery, courage, and
selflessness.*

At every stage in the curating of these history lessons, of interviewing
war heroes and recording their stories, I had family, friends, and professional colleagues encouraging me. As usual, with our Life Lessons book
series, I was blessed with my wife, Carla, who served as the first filter for
writing tone and content. She helped me stay humble, on point, and
dedicated to the larger duty of honoring our beloved Veterans.

Thanks to Rick Rinehart at Taylor Trade Publishing for believing
in this particular book and understanding the significance. His leadership gives us the "ready all, row"—energizing the Life Lessons team
with timely command.

To Emily Tyler, for her keen editing skills. You made a difference
with this important book.

The passion and drive of Melissa McComas, my literary agent, is second to none. As part of a fifth generation military family, Melissa truly
understood the timeliness of this book and the "heart of the matter."

The cover design of this book and of our Life Lessons series is gracefully accomplished by the talented Julia Hulling. She has a rare combination of sense and sensibility.

To my mother, Lieutenant Mary "Petie" Petrick Tocquigny, who singularly taught me to honor Veterans, salute the flag, hold my hand over my heart for "The Star-Spangled Banner," and shout the Pledge of Allegiance (especially the phrase "One Nation Under God"), I thank you.

For Bob Patrick and his incredible team at the Veterans History Project. They have gathered more than one hundred thousand stories from America's Veterans and have been a constant source of stories.

To Val Nicholas for his vision and support behind this book. His leadership and ability to rally a nation behind our Veterans is truly remarkable.

We thank Got Your Six, Hiring Heroes, and the American Legion for their wonderful support.

Finally, we appreciate all the story contributors and their relatives. We encourage all Americans associated with Veterans to capture their history and send them to the Veterans History Project.

Introduction

Memories of destructive wars and conflicts fade as time flies by. Within six short years, taps will be played for the last living Veteran of World War II. Three years ago, we honored the last Veteran of the first great war: World War I.

Life Lessons from Veterans is a tribute book with the intention of getting Americans to stop, listen, and thank our living Veterans for serving our country. We can rely only on history and history must be remembered. At danger is the chance that these wars and conflicts will become abstract to the next generation. If you don't understand and appreciate history, another world war may just happen again.

The aim of this book is to plant a seed in the collective consciousness of America. Remember our Veterans, remember why they defended our country, honor their courage, bravery, duty, and purpose . . . and don't assume that a war could not happen again. Using this book and the Veterans History Project as a launching pad, stop and appreciate our Veterans and the history that they made. Do not let the American human record involving our Veterans become littered with lessons unlearned.

~

Writing History

The Veterans History Project

When the Library of Congress began collecting the oral histories of American war Veterans back in 2002, the primary goal was to preserve history. Since then, thousands of Veterans have been interviewed and the audio and video of those interviews stored in the library's permanent Veterans History Project collection, including an interview from Francis Resta by the students of DaVinci High School.

Francis Resta wasn't supposed to be in the war. "I was considered 4-F because my eyes were bad," Resta told the students, but his father, a career military man, found a doctor to cheat and get Resta cleared, "because no son of his was going to be 4-F." Resta was mentally returning some 70 years to the battlefields of Europe, where he found himself immersed in combat as a 17-year-old U.S. Army soldier.

"After Pearl Harbor," he said, "the guys were all expected to join. I was a sophomore in high school in 1941 and it was just no question." So Resta soon found himself in war-torn France, part of the Allied effort to cross the Rhine into Germany and at long last end the war. It took months to go some 50 miles, and thousands of American soldiers died in the process. Resta himself was wounded and nearly lost his leg. "Going into battle for the first time was scary, of course. There was very little communication. We didn't know where we were. After being in combat for a while, we didn't know what day it was. We didn't have billets . . . we didn't have regular meals. You ate when you were hungry. We had no idea that we would be living like animals."

Resta said many decades after the war, an Iraq War Veteran asked him what sort of beds they slept in during World War II. "I thought that was strange," he said with a laugh, "because we just had over-coats."

"We were always tired. We never got enough sleep. . . . Most of us were numb emotionally. "I got a nickname," Resta said. "'Mole,' be-cause the German mortar shells made little holes and I tried to get in one when we were first shelled because I was scared."

Of camaraderie, Resta said, "When you're building a house with a crew, and someone needed something, he yelled for it. In combat, no one asked for help . . . but if you saw a need, you help. All of us together is one person. We know helping everybody else was the only way to stay alive. You knew your survival depended on the people around you." Resta reinforced that "In combat, you don't have feel-ings. You have to change yourself into an entirely different human being, not even a human being. I learned how fragile the self-image of your self is, how you can believe you're a good person, then find out that you're not."

"We were taught to be angry," he said. "When combat soldiers come back home, that's one thing you can count on: They're angry. You survive combat because you're angry." But they've also learned to sup-press their feelings, he said, so much so that his own children told him years later they didn't think he loved them because he never showed any emotion. And he never talked to his family about what he'd been through.

Combat Veterans, he said, want their loved ones to understand what they're going through, but they don't want to burden them. "It's a dilemma every soldier understands," he said. Even during combat, his letters home to his family contained no details of the horror he was experiencing. "They didn't even know I was in combat because you just don't write about it," Resta said. "I wrote mostly about the other guys . . . chess tournaments . . . the German towns."

That habit of keeping everything inside finally came to an end in 1992, Resta said, when he realized he needed help for his post-traumatic stress disorder and sought it from the Veterans Administration. He participates in regular group therapy with other combat Veterans to this day, and has written a book about PTSD as well, *The Combat Veteran and PTSD, and Help for the Family.* "The military makes the PTSD issue seem much smaller than it is," [Da Vinci student David] Steele said later. "When it's actually almost a guarantee that you'll need some sort of therapy afterwards."

At the end of the battle, write the history of our nation by inter-viewing Veterans, learning everything . . . even about their emo-tional scars.

∽

"Always remember, if you have [emotional scars from war], it is not a sign of weakness; rather it is proof of your strength, because you survived." —Michel Templet

Adapted from an interview with World War II Veteran Francis Resta for the Library of Congress, as reported by Anne Ternus-Bellamy in the *Davis Enterprise* (January 7, 2014).

~

THE HEART OF VETERANS

~

Life Lesson #1

Our Squadron Janitor

William Crawford was an unassuming, humble man, who could be easily overlooked during a hectic day at the U.S. Air Force Academy. Old Bill was the squadron janitor.

While cadets busied themselves preparing for academic exams, athletic events, Saturday morning parades, room inspections, and never-ending leadership classes, Bill quietly moved about mopping and buffing floors, cleaning toilets, or just tidying up the mess of 100 college-age kids.

For many years, only a few cadets gave Bill much notice, rendering little more than a passing nod or muttering a "G'morning" in his direction as they hurried off. Why? Perhaps it was because of the way he did his job, always keeping the squadron area spotlessly clean. As a matter of fact, he did his job so well, none of the students had to notice or get involved. After all, cleaning toilets was his job, not the cadets.

Maybe it was his physical appearance that made him invisible. Bill didn't move very quickly and even shuffled a bit, as if he suffered from some sort of old injury. Bill was practically a senior citizen working in a young person's world. Anyway, what could he have to offer the cadets on a personal level?

Bill was very shy, almost painfully so, seldom speaking to a cadet unless they addressed him first, always burying himself in his work. The

Academy, one of our nation's premier leadership laboratories, kept every cadet busy from dawn till dusk. As for the elderly Bill . . . well, he was just a squadron janitor.

That changed one fall Saturday afternoon when a cadet was reading about World War II and the tough Allied ground campaign in Italy. He stumbled across an incredible story.

William Crawford "in the face of intense and overwhelming hostile fire . . . with no regard for personal safety . . . on his own initiative . . . single-handedly attacked fortified enemy positions. . . . For conspicuous gallantry and intrepidity at risk of life above and beyond the call of duty . . ."

"Holy cow . . . our janitor [may be] a Medal of Honor [recipient]." With great anticipation, the squadron met Bill bright and early Monday morning showing him the page from the book. He stared at it for a few silent moments and then quietly uttered something like, "Yep, that's me." Mouths agape, we humbly asked, "Why didn't you ever tell us about it?" He slowly replied after some thought, "That was one day in my life and it happened a long time ago."

Things were never quite the same around the squadron. Word spread like wildfire among the cadets that they had a hero in their midst. Mr. Crawford, squadron janitor, had been bestowed The Medal! Cadets who had once passed by Bill with hardly a glance now greeted him with a smile and a respectful, "Good morning, Mr. Crawford."

Those who had before left their mess for the "janitor" to clean up started taking it upon themselves to put things in order. Almost overnight, Bill went from being a janitor in our squadron to Mr. Crawford, one of the squadron's teammates.

Mr. Crawford changed too, moving with more purpose, his shoulders a bit more upright, meeting us with a direct look and a stronger "good morning" in return, and flashing his crooked smile more often. While no one ever formally acknowledged the change, the squadron became Mr. Crawford's own corps of cadets.

A very wise person once said, "It's not life that's important, but those you meet along the way that make the difference." Bill Crawford, the Squadron Janitor, taught many valuable, unforgettable leadership lessons, but none more important than this—if a Medal of Honor recipient could clean latrines and smile, is there a job beneath your dignity?

> Life is a leadership laboratory . . . you can learn outside of a class-room. And at the end of the battle, never miss the opportunity to learn from leaders in all levels of life.

William Crawford, a Medal of Honor recipient for his heroic actions during World War II, retired from the army and worked as a janitor at the U.S. Air Force Academy so that he could remain close to the military. He passed away in 2000.

Adapted with permission from Colonel James E. Moschgat, United States Air Force, Retired.

~

Life Lesson #2

The School Desks

In September of 2005, a social studies schoolteacher from Arkansas did something not to be forgotten. On the first day of school, with permission of the school superintendent, the principal, and the building supervisor, she took all of the desks out of the classroom. The kids walked into first period, and there were no desks. In surprise, they looked around and said, "Where's our desks?" The teacher said, "You can't have a desk until you tell me how you earn them." They thought, "Well, maybe it's our grades." "No," she said. "It's our behavior?" And she told them, "No, it's not even your behavior."

As the day progressed, students would file into the classroom and encounter the "no desk room." By early afternoon television news crews had gathered in the class to find out about this crazy teacher who had taken all the desks out of the classroom. The instructor gathered her students during the last period of the day. This time students were sitting on the floor around the sides of the room, and the teacher began class with: "Throughout the day no one has really understood how you earn the desks that ordinarily sit in this classroom. Now I'm going to tell you."

She went over to the door of her classroom and opened it, and as she did twenty-seven U.S. Veterans, wearing their uniforms, walked into that classroom, each one carrying a school desk. They placed those school desks in rows, and then they stood along the wall. By the time they had finished placing the desks, those kids, for the first time in their lives, understood.

Their teacher said, "You don't have to earn those desks. These guys did it for you. They put them out there for you, but it's up to you to sit here responsibly, to learn, to be good students and good citizens, because they paid a price for you to have that desk. Don't ever forget it."

At the end of the battle, remember the little things that you enjoy with the freedom of the United States, all brought to you by your Veterans.

∼

"A freedom that only asks what's in it for me, a freedom without love, duty or patriotism, is unworthy of our founding ideals and those who died in their defense." —President Barack Obama

~

Life Lesson #3

Mother Lode

When the devastating news came from Afghanistan of Mike's death, it was overwhelming. The McMahons were both military officers and had shared everything: child care, cooking, practically every task. They would split a few jobs at home, like Mike filing the tax return, but the rest of life was strictly 50/50, equally yoked as two oxen.

Mike was her partner, best friend, and coparent of "My Three Sons." When Mike was deployed, she struggled just to keep up with all of the things needed to run the household. Most importantly, the boys were going through their own struggles without their dad, especially now.

With the loss of Mike, Jeanette moved the family to West Point and had her last assignment in the army there, serving as the special assistant to the superintendent for human relations and diversity. Eventually she retired from the service after many years of dedication to her country.

Financially, Jeanette was doing fairly well with a pension and non-taxable benefits. Considering herself an unusual war widow with a more senior husband, older children, and the anticipation of college for the three sons, it was a true necessity to save for their education. Until a certain intersection occurred, Jeanette never considered applying for financial assistance.

Then, General David Petraeus was scheduled to be the speaker at Jeanette's oldest son's (Mike Jr.) high school graduation. Having moved so much, Mike never liked school. He had ADHD and was older than most of the other children. It had been a hard journey.

Jeanette was used to writing speeches and she e-mailed General Petraeus's speechwriter. She explained that "academically Mike is probably the second to last student. It would mean a lot to Mike to be acknowledged for his persistence in the context of having lost his dad in Afghanistan. Petraeus followed through and acknowledged Mike Jr. in the graduation speech. Afterward, Petraeus's wife told Jeanette about the Children of Fallen Patriots Foundation and how it provides college scholarships to children who have lost a parent to combat.

Jeanette was just listening and then said, "Oh, that's great, so many people really need help. We'll be okay, though." General Petraeus said, "The point is not how much you have or how much you put away; we feel that we as a country owe this to you. Colonel McMahon, I'm giving you an order," he said. "I want you to sign those boys up for those scholarships."

Jeanette did. And that is one of the things that has really helped make things easier for her family. The Children of Fallen Patriots has provided a timely benefit and service to "Her Three Sons." Being a single parent, the responsibilities are not easy.

Every day presents its own new set of mother lode challenges. The certainty is that tomorrow, you get up and do it all over again . . . perhaps a little better than before.

At the end of the battle, others are willing to help you. Just ask.

⁓

"We owe our Veterans a debt we can never repay." —Doc Hastings

~

Life Lesson #4

Duty, Honor, Loyalty

Many people know what the words *loyalty*, *duty*, *honor* and *selfless service* mean. How often do you see someone, much less a whole community, actually live up to those values?

Entering the military in 1974, Val Nicholas raised his hand and took an oath to protect his nation. His unit also promised to protect each other and never leave a comrade behind. After he left the service, his hand never went down and the commitment to protect America with duty, honor, and loyalty in a selfless manner is more significant today than ever. Starting from day one in basic training, Nicholas learned important army values that would become embedded in his DNA:

1. Be mission oriented: specific plans are detailed, placing the mission first.
2. Act as a team: a mission is never accomplished alone.
3. Never quit: your team can't be in the middle of a firefight and call time out.

In his second stint of army education, Nicholas completed advanced training on the most updated communication gear, accessible only to the U.S. military. As assignments were called out, most of his 250 colleagues went to Vietnam. He, however, was sent to Fulda Gap,

Germany, on the Cold War border of East and West Germany, intersecting NATO and communism. As a member of the 11th Armored Cavalry Regiment, Nicholas ran communication security for the entire regiment, living under the motto "If you can't communicate, you can't command." Every single member of the team was important, from the mechanics who changed transmissions to the drivers of huge M88 tanks who pulled other tanks out of the mud. Everybody had a function in an environment where there was no such thing as a small job.

On a mission to qualify tank crews through night maneuvers, Nicholas's team hit specific infrared-lit targets. Raining like hell, in pitch black darkness, six foot wide mud holes cratered the ground entombing the M88s. With a finite amount of time to get their tasks completed, a decision to improvise was made on the spot. Everyone jumped in to attach cables from tank to tank, pulling each other out of the craters. It was mission accomplished through teamwork and a never-quit attitude.

Transitioning in 1976 to civilian life, Nicholas won a television scholarship while in college under the G.I. Bill. When he first started, he was producing a morning talk show, five days a week, one hour per day. His staff consisted of two anchors, one assistant, and himself as producer. For three years, Nicholas was responsible for most of the supportive roles. What he didn't realize at the time was that it was impossible for one person to do *all* activities to produce a show. Nicholas persevered and never quit.

In the 1990s, Safe Streets was launched in Tacoma, Washington, as the community mission to take back the streets from drug dealers. Nicholas was part of the local NBC affiliate and worked closely with the Tacoma organization. Drug dealers in one particular neighborhood were using a huge mountain of dirt in the middle of an empty lot for transactions. Tacoma citizens had tried forever to get the mound of dirt moved, but to no avail.

Nicholas called the commanding officer (CO) of the local Army Corps of Engineers and told him about the mound. In an instant, the CO blurted: "Have your camera crew out there tomorrow morning and film our bulldozers leveling the hill." City officials arrived and told the CO "you can't do that without a permit." With news cameras rolling, the CO asked, "Would you like for me to put it back?" The city officials acquiesced, and witnessed army corps action as the turning point to transforming Tacoma. It was mission accomplished with great teamwork.

In 2012, Kevin Schmeigel, a Marine Veteran from the National Chamber of Commerce, approached Nicholas about getting NBC involved in some Veteran job fairs that he was starting. Out of that initial meeting, Hiring Our Heroes was born. The chamber does the heavy lifting while NBC *Nightly News, The Today Show,* MSNBC, and local stations across the country bring Veterans and hiring companies together. To date, 250,000 Veterans have attended over eight hundred job fairs across the country. Thirty thousand Veterans have been hired from various companies and franchises. NBC Universal has hired 3,700 Veterans, more than tripling their initial employment goal.

Nicholas's dream is that every company, big or small, will establish a Veterans' network. It will be mission accomplished when he sees every Veteran hired for a job.

At the end of the battle, count on Veterans to keep their oath and become America's next greatest generation of community builders.

⁓

"World II Veterans were truly the greatest generation, but this current group of Veterans who have deployed five or more times are the NEXT greatest generation. With a sense of duty, honor and loyalty, these are the people that our country can lean into."
—Val Nicholas

Veterans Day

We honor you, who fought for us,
for country's sake of freedom's plight.
You kept the greatest country great,
by sacrifice of you who served.

Honor to military, soldiers served.
There seems no risk in peace to serve.
When war breaks the silent peace,
no peace when security cease.

Sacrifice of civilian life,
careers succumb to enlist, or draft.
Families wait in fear, in prayer,
for loved ones return alive, not dead.

Returned Heroes and those deceased,
we honor, thank, though insufficient.
Parades, programs, our pride convey,
we honor you on Veterans Day.

~

Life Lesson #5

War Pierces the Soul

Young men and women enter into a bloody conflict with all five senses. They see the ravages of a war. They hear searing bullets at the tip of their nose while their commanding officer calls the battle cry. They can smell fear and taste victory. The experience pierces to the division of their soul and spirit, down to the marrow of their bones. With an unshakable confidence that their job needs to be completed, they draw strength from one another and from God above. They desire that each man in their unit show equal earnestness to the task at hand. There cannot be any sluggishness if the oppressor is to be defeated.

They are American soldiers, brave and true. Heirs to the promise of the unchangeable character holding steadfastly to hope . . . surely God will not overlook their work and provide some hedge of protection for those fighting the great enemy of the day.

Veterans look back with enlightenment of the struggles they endured. They don't expect us to fully understand the depths of their experience, but simply acknowledge their service with a simple thank you.

At the end of the battle, war takes all of you and even more.

～

"You gifted us by preserving our freedom. Your enduring spirit will never ever fail you."

Inspired by Hebrews 10:2.

~

Life Lesson #6

Size of the Heart

Over a few weeks of difficult training, William McRaven's SEAL class, which started with 150 men, was down to just 35. There were now six boat crews of seven men each. There was a boat with the tall, flexible guys. The most unassuming, prolific boat crew was made up of the little guys, the munchkin crew. No one was over five foot five. The munchkin boat crew had one American Indian, one African American, one Polish American, one Greek American, one Italian American, and two tough kids from the Midwest farmland.

They out-paddled, out-ran, and out-swam all the other boat crews. The big, muscular men in the other boat crews would always make good-natured fun of the tiny little flippers the munchkins put on their tiny little feet prior to every swim. But somehow these little guys, from every corner of the nation and the world, always had the last laugh—swimming faster than everyone and reaching the shore long before the rest of the class.

SEAL training was a great equalizer. Nothing mattered but the will to succeed. Not your color, not your ethnic background, not your education, and not your social status.

At the end of the battle, measure a person by the size of their heart, not the size of their flippers.

～

"It's not the size of the dog in the fight, it's the size of the fight in the dog." —Mark Twain

Adapted from Admiral McRaven's commencement speech delivered at the University of Texas at Austin on May 17, 2014.

~

Life Lesson #7

War and the Textbook Education

One day, eighteen-year-old teenagers were lugging their textbooks and the next day they were carrying weapons on their young shoulders in order to protect our nation and preserve our freedom. The sacrifices they made changed their lives and teenage experiences, and in turn, made ours better. A World War II Veteran was quoted as saying, "Experience is a hard teacher because she gives the test first and the lesson afterwards." Each and every Veteran obtained experience the hard way and then learned the lessons of life:

- They learned geography by traveling to foreign lands that they would have only learned about through textbooks.
- They learned a foreign language from conversations with the citizens in these countries.
- They studied biology through the medical attention they offered their fellow soldiers when they were wounded.
- Their psychology lessons came from sharing compassion when their comrades died in their arms.
- In the subject of history they not only learned it, they *made* history, and we are the recipients of the world they saved.

At the end of the battle, war became the soldiers' classroom.

～

"Like the old soldier of that ballad, I now close my military career and just fade away, an old soldier who tried to do his duty as God gave him the light to see that duty." —General Douglas MacArthur

HEROICS

~

Life Lesson #8

Remember Bataan

Mary "Petie" Petrick had the opportunity to discover and use her God-given talent, which she might not have discovered were it not for her military service. In the absurd combat in the Pacific Theater, she ceased to be just an army nurse from Fredericktown, Pennsylvania, and became an American comrade, equal in the dangerous footing of Bataan, Philippines, trying to survive the cruelty of World War II.

At the time, Petie could not comprehend the profound, transforming power of the Bataan Death March. Willingly volunteering to fly to the Pacific Theater, she put herself in harm's way to help save the lives of the sick and wounded, especially those soldiers brutally punished and starved by the Japanese. For Petie, it was simply a matter of love of country and love for human beings. It was her duty.

For months, the American and Filipino troops fought bravely as the war situation worsened. By April 3, 1942, the Japanese received sufficient reinforcements and began to drive down the Bataan peninsula. Four days later, the Japanese broke through Allied lines. After holding off the Japanese from December to April— four long months—the battle for Bataan ended on April 9th.

Following the fall of the Bataan Peninsula, the United States surrendered to the Japanese, and instantly, more than 75,000 U.S. and Filipino soldiers were forced to become prisoners of war. In total,

10,000 men—1,000 Americans and 9,000 Filipinos—died during the Bataan Death March. Those who survived the march would spend the next forty months in horrific conditions in confinement camps. Most soldiers were transported to Japan aboard "death ships." Given very little food, water, and even clothing, the men were tortured, malnourished, and riddled with disease. Two-thirds would die from disease, starvation, horrendous conditions, and beatings. More than 11,500 American soldiers died during that period of confinement.

Along the sixty-five-mile march to the camp, the Japanese showed no mercy to anyone. If Americans or Filipinos would fall down and couldn't go any further, the Japanese would either bayonet or shoot them. Those who stepped out of line or had fallen out of ranks were beaten with clubs and/or rifle butts. Some American prisoners who couldn't keep up were run over by Japanese vehicles. Many witnessed the remains of an American soldier who had been run over by a tank. The Japanese just left his remains in the middle of the road for all the prisoners to see as they stumbled by.

Wounded American soldiers were expected to keep up like everyone else, regardless of their condition. But some wounded prisoners just couldn't go on. They were either bayoneted, beat with clubs, rifle butts, or shot.

It wasn't until late summer of 1945 that these prisoners of war would see freedom. Survivors were diseased and frail. Men were emaciated, skin and bones, some blind, others unable to walk. Sadly, one-third of the former POWs would die of complications within their first year of freedom. Willingly, Petie Petrick and a group of armed forces nurses stepped up to help save the lives of the sick and wounded, especially those punished and starved soldiers from the Bataan Death March.

At the end of the battle, love of country means sacrifice.

⁓

"I didn't know how to appreciate the good ole USA or know I loved her until I got away." —Henry Trollinger McNutt (Veterans History Project)

"Nurses deserve our gratitude and a place in our national memory and hearts. All told, 59,283 army nurses volunteered to serve in World War II. The author's mother, Petie Petrick, was one of them. She served with 30,000 other nurses in combat zones. Sixteen were killed by enemy action, 201 lost their lives to illness or accident, 1,600 were decorated for meritorious service and bravery under fire."

"Never before have I felt a sense of achievement nor felt that my own bit of work was worth something to somebody. But it is here that our boys are so absurdly grateful for every little affection." —Nettie Eurith Trax, Army Nurses Corps

~

Life Lesson #9

Adapt and React

Iowa native Jim Kleckner entered the U.S. Air Force loaded with bravery, grit, and some single-prop flying experience. He was taught to fly without a radio or lights, preparing him in a raw sort of way for an all-weather inceptor squadron in Germany. In the early 1950s, America's military attention turned to Europe where a new kind of threat showed up on our radar. Hundreds of Russian bombers were ready for takeoff along a two-thousand-mile front, poised to fly west in any condition, at any time during the day. Leadership at the Pentagon determined that the Russian military would advance on Western Europe between 1954 and 1956. This projection drove the Cold War efforts to be combat ready, spearheading four all-weather squadrons to fly the newest jets designed to intercept Russian bombers.

Due to the growing Russian threat, the air corp was made up of World War II captains and young second lieutenants. Kleckner went through initial pilot training in Greenville, Mississippi. On his way to Germany for deployment, he co-commanded the troops with Tom Stafford, a future astronaut in the National Aeronautics and Space Administration. Once in Germany, Kleckner was assigned to the 525th Squadron.

Planning was essential, but the pilot's contingency plans were critical. Kleckner relied on operation orders to guide missions, banking on intelligence data, presumably accurate and timely, to guide them. "You had to know your aircraft, know your environment, and always have a backup plan."

As for his aircraft, Kleckner was one of the first one hundred pilots to fly the F-104. Designed, built, and operable within one year, this Lockheed jet came with a high tail, too tall for an upward ejection seat. Consequently, all F-104s were equipped with a downward ejection seat that was not rocket propelled. Many pilots had lost their lives from this "backwards" ejection. During a night mission in Northern California, Kleckner was the number two jet to take off, with the lead jet ahead of him by one minute. Forming a rectangular flight pattern, the F-104s were in a high-density traffic area headed near San Francisco. Kleckner heard an explosion and lost power.

Knowing that he had only seconds to react, he pulled out a flashlight and checked his altimeter and airspeed. Dropping from 1500 to 1200 feet in a matter of seconds, he pulled the RAT handle, but with no response. He then pulled his landing gear handle and nothing happened. Going into emergency mode, Kleckner knew that if his jet slowed to 165 mph, he would go down. Dropping to 800', too low to eject, he rolled the plane 180 degrees (upside down) ejected upward, opposite the engineered procedure, and parachuted into the San Pablo Bay. When Kleckner came face-to-face with Murphy's Law, he quickly adapted and overcame. What was the alternative? Knowing his plane allowed him to think within seconds and survive.

Veterans like Kleckner don't view chaos as stressful, but an opportunity to act with decisiveness and distinction.

At the end of the battle, always adapt quickly and improvise.

∿

"There's no room for 'I should have seen that coming' when it comes to a jet that has just exploded." —J. J. Kleckner

~

Life Lesson #10
You Had the Rice Seeds

Dr. Thomas Hargrove often remembered one of the rules for a better life that American author Robert Fulghum used: "Always take the scenic route." It was the last decision he would make for a long time.

Hargrove grew up on a red-dirt, dry-land cotton farm in Rotan, Texas. With his "earthy" background, his school of choice was Texas A&M University. Graduating from the all-male, military school in 1966 with degrees in agricultural science and journalism, he was commissioned a second lieutenant in the United States Army.

Reporting to Infantry Officers School at Ft. Benning, Georgia, in June 1968, he was assigned as an agricultural advisor to Advisory Team 73, Military Assistance Command in Chuong Thien province. Located at the southern tip of Vietnam's Mekong Delta, it was one of the country's most war-torn areas. In addition to his role as junior grade officer, Hargrove advised Vietnam agricultural officials and farmers, traveling mostly by sampans on the muddy, brown rivers and water canals.

In 1967, IR8, a high-yielding variety of rice was introduced. This newly developed variety was nicknamed "the miracle rice" by international media. Hargrove and IR8 turned stagnant farms into high production operations, often tripling the yield overnight. Still a soldier, Hargrove became a friend to the world helping to start the Green

Revolution. There in the murky canals of the Mekong, this second lieutenant sparked his personal interest in fighting starvation around the globe. Driven by this special passion, he never showed a kernel of fear in the face of danger.

Returning to the Mekong Delta in 1988, Hargrove met a former Viet Cong officer who remembered him from the war years. The officer told Hargrove he could have killed him at any time during the war. When Hargrove asked why he hadn't, the officer replied, "Because you had the rice seeds."

Three years after an honorable discharge from the army, Hargrove became a journalist in 1973 with the International Rice Research Institute (IRRI) in Manila, Philippines. Friends jokingly called him a "rice bore," but his work translating complex crop science into plain language helped farmers in developing countries increase their yields. One of his publications through IRRI, "A Farmer's Primer on Growing Rice," was written and distributed in 44 countries in 29 different languages.

Hargrove passed away at age 66. Buried on his family's farm, Aggies from all over came to sing "The Spirit of Aggieland" to celebrate him. Hargrove's life is captured by a simple list on his tombstone that reads: "Farmer, Aggie, Soldier, Scientist, Writer, Survivor, and Master of the Green Revolution."

At the end of the battle, serving your fellow man is your best bid for remembrance.

"The ones among you who will be really happy are those who have sought and found how to serve." —Albert Schweitzer

~

Life Lesson #11

Code Talker

Joseph Oklahombi, born in 1892, from Wright City, has been lauded as Oklahoma's greatest war hero of World War I. Oklahombi left his native Kiamichi Mountains and few neighbors for Idabel, where he would enlist. After basic training, the young Choctaw was sent to France.

A month before the armistice in 1918, Oklahombi and his buddies in Company D, 141st Infantry, 36th Division, were cut off from the rest of the company. They came across a German machine gun emplacement, with about fifty trench mortars. Crossing "No Man's Land" numerous times, the Choctaw warrior assisted his wounded friends and carried information back to headquarters about the enemy. Oklahombi moved about 200 yards over open ground against artillery and machine gun fire, rushing a machine gun nest and capturing one of the guns. Turning the weapon on the enemy, his heroics began a blistering four-day firefight eventually won by the Americans.

On another occasion, Oklahombi confronted a German troop having a meal and resting in a cemetery. Enclosed by high walls with only one gate, Oklahombi covered the gate with rapid fire. A true marksman, Oklahombi killed seventy-nine Germans until the whole force surrendered. Besides his fighting activities in Europe during the war, Oklahombi was valuable to Allied troops because of his Indian background.

Allies used the Choctaw language as a code for messages—a code never broken by the German intelligence officers.

Oklahombi, on returning to his homeland, was another soldier home from the war—no triumphant entry into the port of New York, no bands playing, nor a ticker tape parade. He was merely another soldier from the war making his way back to his home in the Kiamichi Mountains in southeastern Oklahoma to be with his wife and son. Joseph settled back to a life of farming, hunting, and fishing.

> At the end of the battle, serve nobly with your endowed skills.

"I believe much trouble would be saved if we open our hearts more." —Chief Dan George, Choctaw Chief

"If a piece of the United States is molested, we must be prepared to defend ourselves." —Joseph Oklahombi

~

Life Lesson #12

Wings Across America: Heroic WASPs

The story of the Women Airforce Service Pilots (WASP) is a chapter from World War II nearly forgotten for over 30 years. The first American women trained to fly military aircraft, the WASP logged over 60 million miles between 1942 and 1944 ferrying planes, towing targets, testing planes, and training pilots. But they were civil servants, never fully incorporated into the armed forces. In 1977, after air force women began training for the first time to fly planes, Congress passed legislation to belatedly give the true pioneers, the WASP, Veteran status. And in 2009, surviving WASP Veterans were awarded the Congressional Gold Medal.

> "You don't need legislation to prove something . . . you can be whatever you set your heart and head to be, and don't let anybody tell you can't be, because 1078 women pilots did it in World War II." —WASP Annelle Henderson Bulechek, 44-w-2

> "And when the wheels left the ground, I was thereinafter hooked for the rest of my life." —Gayle Dora Bevis Reed (now ninety-six years young)

"You either had a chance of doing it or go home. Those who wanted transfers went home! We did what we were assigned to do . . . with no regrets!" —Ruth Thomason Florey, 43-w-4

"Help me remember, Lord, that nothing is going to happen today that you and I can't handle together."
—Sylvia Dahmes Clayton, 43-w-5

"The main thing in my life is: 'TELL THE TRUTH!' Other than that, just persevere . . . never give up . . . just keep plugging . . . (but) that's what I would say is my one think, TELL THE TRUTH!" —Betty Archibald Fernandes, 43-w-3

"Glamour, hell, it was hard work!"

"My favorite word? Honor! Oh, honor! That to me is more than a word. I mean, that's a way of life. . . . I'd die for honor!"
—Florence Shutsy Reynolds, 44-w-5

"It is natural for a person to seek happiness in life. However, I believe that this desirable aim is never achieved if one attempts to find it directly. Instead, happiness is found indirectly as a by-product from devoted service to the lives of others."
—Marie Mountain Clark, 44-w-1

"How to reach a youngster with the proper words . . . would fail me. . . . I can't know what would reach them. I can only tell them the one thing that somebody told me . . . anything you want to do, you can do . . . anything . . . and *believe it* . . . you can do it. Don't let people tell you you can't . . . don't let people tell you you aren't good enough. *Be good enough.*"
—Gayle Snell, 44-w-9

"Never say 'No.' You might miss something!"
—Lillian Epsberg Goodman, 43-w-5

"You don't need legislation to prove something . . . you can be whatever you set your heart and head to be, and don't let anybody tell you you can't be, because 1078 women pilots did it in World War II." —Annelle Henderson Bulechek 44-w-2

"Do not undervalue your abilities. You have ability that you haven't had a chance to use. Now, find something you want to use 'em on and then get after it!" —Florene Miller Watson, WAFS

"Put God first, family next, and then do whatever you want to do, or whatever's needed. The sky's the limit. When you're needed, be there. You can do anything with God's help." —Marion Stegeman Hodgson, 43-w-5

"Failure is not always failure. Sometimes, it's simply a change in direction. Count your many blessings, and move on!" —Deanie Bishop Parrish, 44-w-4

"How do I feel about being a WASP? Out of nothing, it made me something, because it gave me the courage to try anything! [You've got to] make your own opportunities!" —Charlyne Creger, 44-W-10

". . . we all set our own priorities. As you go through life, maybe your priorities need to be an artist, or maybe a musician, or any field you can think of. It doesn't have to be aviation. If you want to do anything in life badly enough, you can do it!" —Betty Haas Pfister, 43-w-5

"The future holds so much for you. If you can have a goal and dream that you want to fulfill, just do your best, and you'll be able to do it! . . . [but you've got to] set your goals HIGH!" —Sandy Sandford Thompson, 43-w-5

"You want to be the next 'Greatest Generation'? Then, return to the values that we lived by in 1942, 1944: sexual relations are for marriage, marriage is for life, there's a right and a wrong, you are responsible for your own actions . . . and a strong faith in God." —Ruth Dailey Helm, WASP

". . . 100 years from now, none of us is going to be here and there's going to be a whole new generation . . . and if we have not passed on the ideals that make a country, that make a nation, that make a people, then there's not going to be any more people! [As for me, I want my life to be] a legacy of love!"
—Anita Paul (aka Sister Teresa) 44-w-6

". . . if they don't know history, if they don't place any importance on history, we're in trouble, because history is so important . . . not just the history of women, the history of our country!" —Doris Brinker Tanner, 44-w-4

At the end of the battle, heroism is genderless.

～

"This is not a time when women should be patient. We are in a war and we need to fight it with all our ability and ever weapon possible. WOMEN PILOTS, in this particular case, are a weapon waiting to be used." —Eleanor Roosevelt, 1942

~

Life Lesson #13

We Grew Up Overnight at the Battle of the Bulge

Vincil Mares joined the army in 1943 and worked as a medic. "For survival, we had to do what we had to do, and everyone did their job." Serving at the Battle of the Bulge for the forty-one-day offensive, he witnessed America's bloodiest battle of World War II. Mares recalled that "we grew up overnight."

Undermanned and not prepared to camp out in temperatures that dropped to four degrees below zero Fahrenheit, Mares and hundreds of thousands of young American forces held out against German tanks. As the German armies quickly drove deeper into the Ardennes in an attempt to secure vital bridgeheads west of the River Meuse quickly, the line defining the Allied front took on the appearance of a large protrusion or bulge, the name by which the battle would forever be known.

On December 16, 1944, three German divisions made up of 250,000 soldiers launched their most desperate and gory battles of the war in the frigid forest. They caught the Americans by surprise and the once peaceful region became a living hell. When the Nazi commander demanded the surrender of the Americans, Brigadier General Anthony McAuliffe, commander of the 101st Airborne Division, responded with a one-word answer—"Nuts."

Several factors turned the tide for the Allies. Lieutenant General George S. Patton and his soldiers' remarkable feat of turning the U.S. Third Army ninety degrees from Lorraine to relieve the battered town of Bastogne, combined with the Germans running out of fuel and the Russian forces pushing inward, thwarted the Germans' counteroffensive.

The Battle of the Bulge was the costliest action ever undertaken by the U.S. Army with casualties topping 100,000. The Germans lost over 80,000, but . . .

"And at the end of the battle, the people were protected and freedom was preserved by youthful Americans."
—Vencil Mares, active owner of Taylor Café, Taylor, Texas

"The smell of death . . . is something that stays with you for a lifetime." —James Mitsuo Furukawa

"Give me four clear days so that my planes can fly, so that my fighter-bombers can bomb and strafe, so that my reconnaissance may pick our targets for my magnificent artillery. Give me four days of sunshine to dry out this blasted mud, so that my tanks roll, so that ammunition and rations may be taken to my hungry, ill-equipped infantry. I need these four days to send von Rundstedt and his godless army to their Valhalla. I am sick of this unnecessary butchery of American youth, and in exchange for four days of fighting weather, I will deliver you enough Krauts to keep your bookkeepers months behind their work. Amen."
—General George Patton's Prayer

~

Life Lesson #14

M.A.S.H. *Innovation*

Vance D. Funkhouser was a part of a family in the 3rd Air Rescue Squadron during the Korean War. As a staff sergeant, he worked on the front lines to rescue wounded soldiers and helicopter transport the wounded to Mobile Air Surgical Hospital (M.A.S.H.) units. Life on the front line was stressful. North Korean guerrilla fighters were conducting middle of the night attacks, coming into tents and stabbing everyone. The only way to survive was to act like family and protect each other. "Rank didn't seem to matter. Everyone went by their first names, like a big family." As a member of the most decorated outfit in Korea, rank wasn't as important. Working together and saving soldiers was all that mattered.

Trained as a mechanic, Vance recognized a need on board the helicopters for the wounded to receive blood plasma while in transit to the M.A.S.H. unit. The wounded soldiers were carried in litters snapped outside the body of the aircraft. Vance used his aptitude for mechanical devices to create a handmade apparatus for the blood plasma bag to be snapped to the litter. His invention gave injured GIs invaluable in-flight treatment.

Funkhouser worked long hours to make sure that all aircraft was equipped with this device. Two were built onto both sides of each helicopter. (You can see them on M*A*S*H* reruns.) He was awarded the Bronze Star for his in-flight device.

> At the end of the battle, work together as a family to save lives.

∼

"It saved many, many lives. We don't know how many, but we know it did save a lot of lives, because if you can't get blood, you're going to die." —Vance D. Funkhouser

~

IN THE TRENCHES

Life Lesson #15

Far Better to Dare Mighty Things

Chris Kyle, the "American Sniper," had many Veteran heroes in his heart and mind. One in particular, Carlos Hathcock, was a true legend from the Vietnam War. Hathcock taught himself to shoot as a boy, just like Alvin York and Audie Murphy before him. He had dreamed of being a U.S. Marine his whole life and enlisted in 1959 at just 17 years old. Hathcock was an excellent sharpshooter by then. He won the Wimbledon Cup shooting championship in 1965, the year before he would deploy to Vietnam and change the face of American warfare forever.

Deployed in 1966 as a military policeman, Hathcock immediately volunteered for combat and was soon transferred to the 1st Marine Division Sniper Platoon, stationed at Hill 55, South of Da Nang. Once there, Hathcock would earn the nickname "White Feather" because he always wore a white feather on his bush hat, daring the North Vietnamese to spot him. White Feather would achieve his status as the Vietnam War's deadliest sniper in missions.

O six hundred a.m. and O eighteen hundred p.m. were Hathcock's favorite times to strike. This was important when he volunteered for a mission he knew little about. "First light and last light are the best times," he said. "In the morning, they're going out after a good night's rest, smoking, and laughing. When they come back in the evenings, they're tired, lolly-gagging, not paying attention to detail."

He observed this firsthand, at arm's reach, when trying to dispatch a North Vietnamese Army [NVA] general officer. For four days and three nights, he low crawled inch by inch, a move he called "worming," without food or sleep, more than 1500 yards to get close to the general. This was the only time he ever removed the feather from his cap. "Over a time period like that you could forget the strategy, forget the rules and end up dead," he said. "I didn't want anyone dead, so I took the mission myself, figuring I was better than the rest of them, because I was training them."

Hathcock moved to a tree line near the NVA encampment. "There were two twin .51s next to me," he said. "I started worming on my side to keep my slug trail thin. I could have tripped the patrols that came by." The general stepped out onto a porch and yawned. The general's aide stepped in front of him and by the time he moved away, the general was down, the bullet went through his heart. Hathcock was 700 yards away. "I had to get away. When I made the shot, everyone ran to the tree line because that's where the cover was." The soldiers searched for the sniper for three days as he made his way back. They never even saw him.

"Carlos became part of the environment," said Edward Land, Hathcock's commanding officer. "He totally integrated himself into the environment. He had the patience, drive, and courage to do the job. He felt very strongly that he was saving Marine lives." With 93 confirmed kills—his longest was at 2500 yards—and an estimated 300 more, it really wasn't about the killing. "I really didn't like the killing," Hathcock once told a reporter. "You'd have to be crazy to enjoy running around the woods, killing people. But if I didn't get the enemy, they were going to kill the kids over there."

> At the end of the battle, saving American lives was something a great soldier took to heart.

"War is the highest form of struggle for resolving contradictions."
—Mao Tse-tung

~

A Fighter's Lament

I am sitting here thinking
Of things I left behind,
And I'd like to put in writing
What is running through my mind.

We have dug a million ditches
And have cleared 10 miles of ground,
We have drunk our beer and whisky
In every honky-tonk in town.

But there is one consolation,
Gather round while I tell:
"When we die we'll go to heaven,
For we have done our stretch in Hell."

We have built a million kitchens,
For the cooks to burn our beans;
We have stood a million guard mounts,
And we have cleaned the camp latrines.

We have washed a million spuds,
And killed a million snakes and ants,
That have tried to steal our grub.

When our work on earth is ended,
Then our friends on earth will tell;
"When they died they went to Heaven,
For they've done their stretch in Hell."

When the final taps have sounded,
When we lay aside life's cares,
When we stand our last inspection
On those shining golden stairs,
The angels will welcome us,
Their golden harps will play;
And we draw a million canteen checks
And spend them in a day.

It is there we will hear St. Peter
Tell us loudly with a yell:
"Take a seat, you boys from the jungle,
For you've done your stretch in Hell."

(Author Unknown)

~

Life Lesson #16

They Won't Shoot Crazy People

War reporter Ernie Pyle observed some of the craziest characters in the trenches of World War II. One day Ernie was wandering through a dense olive tree grove and came upon an infantryman. Through a casual conversation, he learned that the soldier had already served two years on the front line.

As Ernie described this particular soldier: "His life consisted wholly for the war, for he had always been an infantryman. He survived because the fates were kind to him. He had become hard and immensely wise in animal like ways of self-preservation. He hated war and wanted to go home."

Much to Ernie's surprise, this infantryman was sitting on the edge of his foxhole wearing a black silk opera hat. It looked like the sprawling head piece from *The Phantom of the Opera* with a wide brim and bric-a-brac trim. It belonged to Private Gordon T. Winter. He had found the fancy hat in a torn-down house from a nearby village. The private picked it up and carried it to his foxhole. Winter was overheard saying, "I'm going to wear this in the next attack. The Germans will think that I'm crazy . . . and they are afraid of crazy people."

At the end of the battle, insane wars produce crazy ways to survive.

～

"Coming home is a gigantic relief. You are wrung out, but alive."
—Gordon Winter

~

Life Lesson #17

Semper Fi Leadership

Marine Corp leadership has helped America win wars. To be always faithful, is clear, steadfast, and straightforward. As a United States Marine Corps Logistics Officer, Jeff Clement completed two deployments to Afghanistan leading hundreds of Marines, Soldiers, Sailors, and Airmen on dangerous resupply convoys. Facing insurgents' improvised explosive devices (IED) and ambushes, the self-sacrificing Marines accomplished their mission through leadership skills. "One of the hardest things to do as a leader is to tell one of your Marines to do something that HAS to be done, placing the individual in a tremendous amount of danger. Without hesitation, these Marines jump into a life threatening situation to clear a path of an ambush or carry out another Marine to a MEDEVAC helicopter."

Self-sacrifice for the greater good is also a leadership lesson branded into Marines. "Think about it, going it on your own never works. A team has to act as one. If a platoon simultaneously attacks in two different directions, the team will be split down the middle with each half defeated."

"Marine leadership means confronting a problem differently. We are taught to analyze it, make a decision as a consensus and act as one unit with confidence, conviction and courage. And as a leader, you are a servant first. You exist for the team, taking care of them and ensuring that they have the tools to accomplish the mission. When you acknowledge that it is never about me, but about the team, great things are possible."

Leadership within the Marines is definitely not about being everybody's friend. It's not found in a textbook or in a TED talk. Leadership is straightforward and an earned trust.

At the end of the battle, Semper Fi leadership starts with respect, defines being faithful, and ends in the sum total of your actions.

"Self-sacrifice for the greater good is the hallmark of a leader."
—Jeff Clement

Visit Jeff Clement at www.clementjd.com.

~

Life Lesson #18

True Nods of Recognition

It was the first day of the ground war of Operation Desert Storm, and it was the only combat this Corpsman was to experience in the brief conflict. A native of Milwaukee, Wisconsin, 6 foot, 4 inch, 240 pound Navy Corpsman Anthony Martin was clad in combat gear with heavy chemical protective wear. On February 24, 1991, U.S. Marines of L Company, 3rd Battalion, 9th Marine Regiment were assaulting across the Al Wafra oil field when the Americans came across a large group of Iraqi soldiers waving white flags.

The Americans ran for the safety of their amphibious tractors, followed by the surrendering Iraqis. Martin said the Iraqis pounded on the vehicles' hatches, begging to be let in. "I said, 'Cool, they're going to surrender!' The Marines began frisking them, and the next thing you heard was 'Whoosh! Whoosh!'" said Martin, mimicking the sound of incoming mortar rounds. "They were really hammering us." 82-millimeter mortar rounds exploded around him, but Martin repeatedly ran to the rescue of wounded Marines.

"I was already inside when I heard people yelling, 'Marteen! corpsman!' . . . Why I got out during a mortar attack to treat the wounded, I don't know. But that's my job. I thought, hell, if I run through here I'm going to get hit. But I wasn't," Martin said.

One of the first of the five wounded Marines he treated was Lance Corporal Richard Musicant, one of Martin's closest friends in L Company. The two had spent the previous night talking for more than four hours about home and their families. A jagged piece of shrapnel had cut a massive swath through Musicant's left leg, severing an artery.

Musicant, from Park Ridge, N.J., was in danger of bleeding to death. "Tony grabbed me by the front of my shirt and threw me over his shoulder. When he picked me up, I noticed a giant pool of blood on the ground, about 12 inches wide. Blood was coming out so fast the ground couldn't soak it up. We were going, and I didn't think my leg was coming with us," Musicant recalled.

Martin slung the wounded Marine, along with Musicant's field radio and other battle gear, over his shoulder and ran about 200 meters to the safety of an amphibious tractor. Also dressed out in a chemical protection gear, the Lance Corporal weighed in excess of 200 pounds.

Once in the vehicle, Martin said he used his entire supply of battle dressings and gauze on Musicant's wound, but the bleeding continued. So Martin used scissors to cut up the T-shirt he was wearing and stuffed it against the wound.

More than two years later, the 22-year-old Musicant is still being treated for the wound at the Naval Hospital in Balboa Park. Naturally, he is eternally grateful to Martin for saving his life: "God loves Tony. He ran through the mortar attack to save me and other wounded Marines and never got hit. That can only happen if God loves you. I lost a lot of blood and was told that I actually kicked off, but was revived by the battalion medical officer." Musicant has undergone seven operations on his leg, and Navy doctors say they have four more operations to perform on him before he can be released from active duty.

Not many support troops earn the respect of infantrymen. Tank or helicopter gunship crews may get an occasional nod of recognition from the grunts. But combat corpsmen like Martin are universally respected in the infantry.

At the end of the battle, nods of recognition come through medals, but most importantly, by saving the lives of friends.

"Our Veterans have put their lives on the line to protect the freedoms that we enjoy. They have dedicated their lives to our country and deserve to be recognized for their commitment."
—Judd Gregg

~

Somewhere in the Pacific

Somewhere in the South Pacific, where the sun is like a curse,
Where each long day is followed by another slightly worse,
Where the coral dust blows thicker than the shifting desert sands,
Where the white man dreams of a finer and slightly colder land.

Somewhere in the South Pacific, where a woman is never seen,
Where the sky is never cloudy and the grass is never green.
Where the gooney birds fuss nightly, robbing man of blessed sleep,
Where there isn't any whiskey, and but two cans of beer a week.

Somewhere in the South Pacific, where the sun bakes the ground,
Where ice water is a failure and your skin is slightly brown,
Where you get so tired of eating dehydrated food each day,
Where work is considered a pleasure to pass the time away.

Somewhere in the South Pacific where mosquitoes own the place,
Where the sweat from your brow trickles rapidly down your face,
Where your days are already numbered and your head points to the ground,
And you know that you have headed for the "Last go round."

Somewhere in the South Pacific where the mail is always late,
Where Christmas cards in April are considered up to date.
Where we always have the payroll, but we never get a cent,
Though we never miss the money, for there is no place to get it spent.

Somewhere in the South Pacific, where they say the "trade winds" blow,
Where your thoughts are always drifting to the "one you use to know,"
Where the moon shines nightly and the stars twinkle in the sky,
Where you wish that you could gladly, stop the tears that fill your eye.

Somewhere in the South Pacific, where a battle has been won,
Where the stars and stripes forever will be standing from sun to sun,
Where you talk about the future, planning things that you will do,
And then you stop and wonder when will those plans come true.

Somewhere in the Southern Ocean, where the sea birds moan and cry,
And the lumbering deep sea turtles come upon the shore to die,
Oh, take me back to the United States, the place I love so well,
for the God-forsaken place we are in, is awfully close to hell.

(Author Unknown)

~

Life Lesson #19

Fly through Life with Bravado, Regardless of the Conditions

The All Weather 496th Fighter Interceptor Squadron was made up of a handful of World War II Veteran pilots, created with the mission of being the first combat-ready unit in the Cold War. The Cold War's so-called Iron Curtain was two thousand miles long aligned with over two million Communist soldiers. The year was 1953. Mao had taken over mainland China. The Russians were quickly advancing their nuclear warheads.

The 496th came from everywhere and nowhere. As Tom Wolfe described in *The Right Stuff*, this was "the top of the ziggurat in the short lives as fighter pilots." With the eye of the tiger, each pilot craved the opportunity for air-to-air battles, putting into practice their heroic instincts. In October, in the early missions, the pilots would be flying at 35,000 feet and would be instructed that "a target" was visible at 5,000 feet. The synchronization of the brave pilots and selfless teamwork eventually became a habit.

Completing 700 hours of flight each month, the 496th was issued alert orders to Europe. They would be stationed at Phalsbourg, France, near the Rhine River separating West Germany and the French border. Given the terrible weather conditions, training in formation flying and landings became more important.

How does a squadron operate with three-quarters of the flying days under Instrument Flight Rules? This meant that cloud ceilings were below 1,000 feet and visibility was less than two miles with constant snow or rain. Eventually the norm became strong cross winds, sloppy conditions, and no alternative landing bases. Not all pilots were spared, especially during Alert Duty. Alert Duty occurred when Russian MIGs were active.

J. B. Lang, father of Jim Monk, was one of the fine, young pilots that perished in the line of duty. During an early morning flight, J. B. was experiencing serious radio problems. With his normal tenacity and bravery, J. B. continued his mission in a raging storm. He was approaching Landstuhl in a torrential downpour when he disappeared from the controllers' radar outside of Kaiserslautern. Sadly, a heroic young pilot was lost that day, leaving behind an equally young wife and newborn son.

> At the end of life's runway, fly through all of life's conditions with bravado.

∾

"Live your life with the bravado of a fighter squadron. Light the fire and be the first one off." —Dr. Jim Monk, J. B. Lang's son

~

Rifleman's Creed

This is my rifle. There are many like it, but this one is mine.

My rifle is my best friend. It is my life. I must master it as I must master my life.

My rifle, without me, is useless. Without my rifle, I am useless. I must fire my rifle true. I must shoot straighter than my enemy who is trying to kill me. I must shoot him before he shoots me. I will . . .

My rifle and I know that what counts in war is not the rounds we fire, the noise of our burst, nor the smoke we make. We know that it is the hits that count. We will hit . . .

My rifle is human, even as I, because it is my life. Thus, I will learn it as a brother. I will learn its weaknesses, its strength, its parts, its accessories, its sights and its barrel. I will keep my rifle clean and ready, even as I am clean and ready. We will become part of each other. We will . . .

Before God, I swear this creed. My rifle and I are the defenders of my country. We are the masters of our enemy. We are the saviors of my life.

So be it, until victory is America's and there is no enemy, but peace!

(Major General William H. Rupertus)

~

Life Lesson #20

The Helmet

A combat or battle helmet was typically designed for one use—personal armor to protect the soldiers' heads from shrapnel, fragments, and bullets. Observing captured Germans from World War II, Americans noticed the prisoners of war weren't wearing their helmets. You would never catch an American without priceless head gear.

Considered a trusty friend, American troops have always been taught that their helmet was a very good thing to have around.

The helmet acted as:

- A shovel to dig a foxhole or even a shallow grave for a fallen colleague
- A bowl to cook in
- A pestle to grind corn mesa for code talkers
- A bucket to gather fruit
- A sink to help you take a bath
- The net overwrap from World War II was used to catch things to eat
- A covering too hot in the summer
- Protection too drafty in the winter
- "Our best armor" to save our brains

At the end of the battle, trusty friends come in handy.

～

"God gives his hardest battles to his toughest soldiers adorned with a helmet." —Unknown

~

Life Lesson #21

Too Young

At sixteen, Bill Geroux was too young for the Second World War when he volunteered in 1943, but he was old enough to guard German prisoners of war in a camp outside of Chatham. Oh, the irony.

After the war ended, he joined the Navy and spent 20 years sailing the world's oceans. He was on the HMCS *Iroquois* in 1952 when enemy shore batteries attacked it during the Korean War, killing three and wounding ten—the only Royal Canadian Navy casualties of the war. He endured hardships, to be sure, not least of which was the significant time he spent away from his family, but his attitude was always positive.

In order to earn his wings as a pilot, Albert Potvin went through a series of rigorous tests that still stand out in his mind today as some of the most grueling of his life. He then spent more than five years based in France as a pilot. At only eighteen years young, he began flying jets, carrying the weight of great responsibility with him on every flight.

This was dangerous business. Many friends never returned to base from flights, yet Albert said some of the greatest challenges were those he faced upon arrival back at home after the war ended. "That was probably the most stressful point in my whole life," Al says. "Here I was, qualified to fly a jet. I taught instrument flying and on guidance simulators—I was fully qualified and there wasn't one flying job available here, militarily or commercially."

But Al was adaptable; a fighter pilot must be. He eventually got a job selling office supplies, which was a far cry from the adrenaline-fueled life he'd known. He had a new wife and a baby to feed, however, and he found great success. As an entrepreneur he would go on to design transportation technology for bus fleets in cities across the world. Adaptability and a youthful spirit helped him survive.

> At the end of the battle, thank the strong youth of your country for defense of the freedom you enjoy.

"War is a terrible thing, filled with the darkest aspects of humanity, but people get through it and build strong lives and loving families because of their resiliency, adaptability and light-hearted spirits." —Kristian Partington

"As we pause to remember the ultimate sacrifice of the fallen, it's also important to remember the lessons of those who returned to build our communities." —Kristian Partington

Perhaps in Death I'll Understand

I find myself fighting a war,
My leaders told me was for right,
As leaders always say before
Getting us into one more fight.
The enemies we fight today
Were friends of ours in the past,
But power shifts in a strange way.
Both friends and foes—they never last.
I am just one of the young who
Are called by old to take my turn,
To give my life to duty to
A reason that I'll never learn.
My Mother's photo in my hand.
Perhaps in death, I'll understand.

(Ima Ryma)

~

Life Lesson #22

What's in a Name?

On February 20th, 1942, a team meeting was held before Butch's squadron left the aircraft carrier USS *Lexington*. They were reminded that their mission was simple—win and hold control of the air.

The courageous team was ready. They had been trained to be exceptionally adept at handling their F4F planes and react with split-second accuracy in all conditions. The *Lexington* had been penetrating enemy waters in the Pacific. They had been spotted over 375 miles from the shipping harbor of Rabaul, New Guinea, by a Kawanishi flying boat. While Lieutenant Commander John Thach had the boat destroyed, the enemy had managed to radio the position of the *Lexington*. The enemy was on the way to bomb the *Lexington*.

More than nine Japanese bombers were reported in route. Thach ordered six F4F Wildcats, one of them piloted by Butch, to intercept them. Butch and his wingman spotted the V formation of Mitsubishi "Betty" G4M1 bombers first, and dove head on into them. His four other colleagues were too far away to reach the enemy planes.

Butch's wingman discovered that his own guns were jammed and radioed the untimely news to Butch. With his wingman forced to turn away, Butch stood alone between the *Lexington* and the V formation of Japanese bombers. Without hesitation, Butch went full throttle into the V. With his amazing pinpoint accurate shooting from .50

caliber guns, Butch downed five oncoming bombers using only sixty rounds of ammunition for each plane. In his final attack, he smashed into the port engine side of the last Japanese bomber. From the *Lexington*, the crew witnessed three enemy bombers falling in flames at the same moment.

Just as Butch ran out of ammunition, Thach and the other Wildcats were in range to drive off the rest of the V. In a genuine heroic act, Butch saved the *Lexington* and was awarded the highest decoration of our country, the Congressional Medal of Honor.

Sadly, in November of 1943, Butch was accidentally shot down by a fellow American during a night fighter ops mission near the Gilbert Islands in the Pacific.

Butch's hometown of Chicago would not allow his heroics to ever be forgotten. You can relive Butch's courageous acts at a memorial between Terminals 1 and 2 at an airport named for him—O'Hare.

And his father would be proud of his son and the family name. For Butch O'Hare's father was the infamous lawyer for Alphonso Capone, notorious mob leader of the Windy City. Easy Eddie O'Hare's own infamy came when he decided that his son Butch deserved an untarnished name. Showing his son the difference between right and wrong, Easy Eddie turned in Al Capone to the Feds.

Eddie's life also ended in a blaze, only by gunfire at the intersection of Ogden and Rockwell in the Windy City. In his mind, he had set the record straight about what really matters in life.

At the end of the battle, you leave this world with only your name and reputation.

～

"Proper names aren't necessarily rigid designators."

~

Life Lesson #23

Believable Leadership Works

In the Persian and Gulf Wars, authentic leadership from Generals Schwarzkopf and Cavazos was vital to winning. Their style instilled trust and focus from the battalion commanders down through the ranks.

"We were very thankful that I had a chance to work for Schwarzkopf because he was a tough taskmaster and you had to produce when you work for him. We were happy to stand in the pocket, throw the ball, connect to its target, at least 80 percent of the time."

General Cavazos's style of leadership was nothing short of magic. He was charismatic, but he was also believable because he had been there and done it. And more importantly, he didn't come across as somebody who was trying to have the best division. Cavazos came across as always preparing these men and women to accomplish their mission. In the process, the perception was that the general took care of us as his family with a personal concern for our health.

General Cavazos didn't want to just see you as a battalion commander. He also wanted to see the private and then the sergeant. "Word got around that when Cavazos arrives, you do your business and let the privates and the sergeants do their business, and their business was to answer the general's questions. Your business was to continue the training. With that, he led a paradigm shift."

At the end of the battle, a believable leadership style works.

～

"Never tell people *how* to do things. Tell them *what* to do and they will surprise you with their ingenuity." —General George Patton

~

AFTER THE BATTLE

~

Life Lesson #24

Moving On

Going off to war is a milestone moment. You are leaving behind loved ones and entering into a new chapter of life. Stuff happens in war that scars you beyond shrapnel. Staring at death, looking into your own abyss, is often mortifying. The whole experience can shape the rest of your life . . . or one can enter in and out with a "that was then . . . this is now" mindset.

Second Lieutenant Mary "Petie" Petrick exhibited a "moving on" attitude. Saving soldiers was her business as a flight nurse in the Pacific theater during World War II. Landing at battle sites just days after the conflict to rescue injured soldiers was her duty and job. Petie saw the worst of casualties, comforted the dying, and treated the wounded with little to nothing in terms of medicine and resources.

Her chosen attitude for all was "moving on" . . . getting past the battle, the blood, and the brain damage of war. Moving on doesn't mean you forget about events and people. It just means you have to accept what happened and continue living.

A dentist once told Petie that letting go is like pulling a tooth. When it was pulled out, you are relieved, but how many times does your tongue run itself over the spot where the tooth once was? Probably a hundred times a day. Just because it was not hurting you doesn't mean you did not notice it. It leaves a gap and sometimes you miss it, especially when you need it to chew. It's going to take a while, but it takes time. Should you have kept the tooth? No, because it was causing you too much pain. Just move on and let go.

> At the end of the battle, move on . . . for life is not meant to be traveled backward.

～

"In order to move on, you must understand why you felt what you did, and why you no longer need to feel it." —Mitch Albom

"You will never find your future in a rearview mirror. Keep moving forward." —Petie Petrick Tocquigny

"I will go, and if I perish, I perish." —Inspired by Queen Esther to Army Air Corp flight nurses, answering her country's call many centuries ago

~

Life Lesson #25

Honoring Selflessness

Serving others and love of God have been common threads throughout the lifetime of Chaplain Major Chad Zielinski, but it was his experience in the Air Force that led to his commitment as a priest.

The 354th Fighter Wing deputy wing chaplain was ordained as a bishop of the Fairbanks Catholic diocese in a ceremony December 15th, 2014. The size of his duty is larger than the geographical expanses of Texas, much of which isn't accessible by road. According to the Pacific Air Forces command chaplain, "this is the first time an active-duty Airman has been chosen for a position of this magnitude."

Born in 1964, in Alpena, Michigan, to a schoolteacher father and social worker mother, Chaplain Zielinski said his family was very committed to their faith, attending church and religious education every week. His father would always say "education is a way to a better life."

After graduating from high school and spending a summer in Valdez, Alaska, as a commercial salmon fisherman, Zielinski joined the Air Force in 1983. He was stationed at Mountain Home Air Force Base, Idaho, where he worked in the 366th Supply Squadron. Staying committed to his faith, he spent a lot of time with the Catholic chaplain who ultimately encouraged him to join seminary after his enlistment was up. "Being involved in the chapel program as a young Airman was a huge impetus for me," he said. "The Air Force has a lot of good people and you just push yourself to do the right thing for these great people."

While serving as a reservist in the Air Force, Zielinski was finally ordained a priest. Logistics forced him to separate completely from being enlisted so he could become a chaplain candidate. "I didn't think I'd ever come back to active duty after becoming a priest in 1996, but this wasn't the case," he said.

After serving as a pastor of three parishes for six years, the events of Sept. 11, 2001, changed his outlook on active duty. "A patriotic sense was immediately rekindled within me," Zielinski said. There was a great need for chaplains at the time and Zielinski made the commitment. With multiple deployments to Iraq and Afghanistan, he has covered eighteen combat outposts. "It's a miracle I'm still around today to serve. God obviously had a plan for me as a servant leader."

Doing his duty loyally without thought of recognition or gain, Zielinski had to go a little further and endure a little longer, living out the values of an American soldier.

At the end of the battle, selfless servitude is honored.

"Honor is a matter of carrying, acting and living the values of respect, integrity and selfless service." —Army Values

Adapted from "Through Airmen's Eyes," U.S. Air Force, December 16, 2014.

~

Life Lesson #26

The Darkest Moment

One of their jobs as Navy SEALs is to conduct underwater attacks against enemy shipping. They practice this technique extensively during basic training. The ship attack mission is where a pair of SEAL divers are dropped off outside an enemy harbor and then they swim underwater for two miles using nothing but a depth gauge and a compass to get to their target.

During the entire swim, even well below the surface, there is some light that comes through. To the trainees, it is comforting to know that there is open water above you. But as they approach the ship, tied to a pier, the light begins to fade. The steel structure of the ship blocks all ambient light.

To be successful in their mission, the SEALs have to swim under the ship and find the keel, the centerline and the deepest part of the ship. This is also the darkest part of the ship, where one cannot see your hand in front of your face. The darkest point is also the most deafening with ship machinery. Attacking all the senses, this is the common point of failure and maximum disorientation.

Every SEAL knows that under the keel, at the darkest moment of the mission, is the time when you must be calm and composed. To survive, all of your tactical skills, physical power, and inner strength must be brought to bear.

At the end of the battle, being your very best in the darkest moment means survival.

～

"You never know how strong you are until being strong is all you have." —Unknown

Adapted from Admiral William McRaven

~

Life Lesson #27

Undercurrent of True Leadership

Submerged with one hundred and ten sailors aboard for over sixty days at a stretch, without surfacing or even exchanging air with the atmosphere, what would leadership look like? What would it take to be successful as a young junior officer and leader in your early twenties?

Submarine leadership was in Bob Viney's family lineage. His dad, John Viney, commanded the USS *Menhaden*. Born into a military family, Bob knew the Naval Academy was his college destination because his dad graduated from there in 1946. John Viney enlisted in the navy in 1941 as a teenager, immediately following the attack on Pearl Harbor, and served as a gunner's mate on board the USS *Vincennes*, a heavy cruiser.

John Viney left the *Vincennes* in June of 1942 to enter NAPS, and then entered the Naval Academy in June of 1943 with the class of 1947. His classmates included former President Jimmy Carter; long-serving senior prisoner of war in North Vietnam, Jeremiah Denton, who became a U.S. senator; and James Stockdale, a Medal of Honor recipient and the vice presidential candidate with Independent candidate for president Ross Perot.

Bob Viney spent his first birthday at the Naval Academy where his father was an instructor in the Navigation Department. He spent his first Christmas at the Submarine School where his father was a student, training for a career as a submarine officer. When Bob was ten years old, his dad became a submarine commanding officer (CO), leading eighty officers and men aboard the USS *Menhaden*. Going to sea for six months at a time, communication with family was essentially nonexistent. There was no electronic communication in those years . . . no e-mail, no texts, no Internet. They had no idea of his dad's whereabouts. When he was gone, he was *totally* gone. It was Bob's mother who led the family of five children to religious education classes, ball games for Bob and his three brothers, and dance recitals for his sister. When he was home, his dad would reintegrate into the family and take over duties that his mom had handled. Overcoming a vision deficiency, Bob graduated from the academy with merit in June 1970, was commissioned an ensign, and accepted for training as a nuclear submarine officer.

In January of 1972, after eighteen months of Nuclear Power and Submarine School training, he reported aboard the USS *Tautog*, home-ported in Pearl Harbor, Hawaii. Bob had recently been promoted from ensign to lieutenant JG (junior grade), and was assigned immediate and significant responsibilities. With the combination of what he learned from his dad, four years at the Naval Academy, and completion of the Nuclear Submarine Power School, Bob grasped his undercurrent role . . . *inspire others to achieve a mission with a purpose that goes beyond personal benefits or rewards.*

What was the undercurrent? Ship culture started with immense respect for each other and a sense of unity within the crew.

- Being a servant leader was all about leading by personal example.
- Everything is always about the crew and not about me.
- Missions are accomplished only through teamwork.

Bob completed certification as Officer of the Deck, where he had responsibility for the overall direction of the USS *Tautog* while at sea. In August of 1972, the ship was engaged in a "one-on-one" training mission outside of Guam for the ballistic missile submarine group based there. The exercise involved the *Tautog* playing the role of a Russian sub that was lying outside the Guam harbor. Their mission: pick up and trail one of the U.S. ballistic submarines leaving port for a Cold War Deterrent patrol.

The *Tautog* CO started the exercise as the "Officer of the Deck." In a designated operating area covering several thousand square miles of the ocean, they lost sonar contact with their target and proceeded to begin a search pattern. After thirty minutes, the CO turned over the command of the ship during the exercise to Bob. The CO went to the wardroom (officer's dining room) to visit with the commodore of the ballistic missile submarine squadron, who happened to be a Naval Academy classmate.

Bob's first tactical move was to reach out to his chief sonarman. He asked the chief to join him in the control room to view the charts. "If you were on the ballistic missile submarine, where would you direct the ship to avoid detection?" After reviewing water depth and temperature and salinity conditions, the chief recommended one part of the operational training area. Bob directed the ship to head to that area. While the chief went off to the sonar room to supervise the sonar search, Bob was directing the ship and the crew of over one hundred sailors. Together they maneuvered the ship to the target. They detected the target and successfully maintained contact for the duration of the exercise. Bob contacted the CO and told him that they acquired the target on passive sonar. The CO was very pleased, but the commodore was incredulous; he wanted to know how the team did it!

Bob told them: "I asked for and followed the Chief's judgment." He had 100 percent trust in the chief's professional skill and expertise as a sonarman thoroughly understanding test depth, water salinity, undersea profile chart interpretation, water depth variations, and identifying where it would be most difficult to pick up sound. The chief had fifteen years of expertise in understanding sound traveling through water.

To Bob, leadership was not about being the most knowledgeable member on the submarine's team. Leadership meant knowing how to get the knowledge, ask the right questions, in combination with the experience to ensure that the mission is accomplished.

By deflecting the mission's success to the chief, Bob built mutual trust and respect with the sub's team. His reliance on the judgment of other, more knowledgeable, members of his team did not diminish his standing in the eyes of the crew. Quite to the contrary, the demonstration of trust and respect for the team raised their own levels of trust and respect for his leadership. These core values allowed Bob's team to consistently perform at a high level of success. Empowering his team to make decisions often required risks, but to Bob, no great result was ever achieved without some level of risk.

"I believe that effective leadership starts with the premise that I'm not the smartest person on my team. Effective leadership means getting input from the experts within the team. Respect others enough to truly value their input. Build trust first and your team will be empowered in an authentic way. In the Navy and in life, if you want respect from others, you have to respect them first."

> At the end of the battle, the undercurrent of leadership moves through trust.

"Leadership is the art of achieving greater results than the science of management says is possible." —General Colin Powell

"Serving on a nuclear sub is 99% boredom and routine and 1% sheer panic. . . . When you have a problem, your life is at risk." —Robert Viney

"Leadership is the art of getting others to do something you want done because they want to do it." —Dwight D. Eisenhower

~

Life Lesson #28

Enlightening Afghans Her Way

Major Mary Clark, a UH-1N Huey instructor pilot and the 58th Operations Support Squadron's assistant director of operations, knows what it takes to make a good helicopter pilot, but also how to enlighten others.

Contributing to the growing Afghan air force, Clark trained pilots at Shindand Air Base, Afghanistan. She prepared 20 student pilots, including three female members of the Afghan air force and male rotary-wing pilots to fly the Russian-made Mi-17, and contributed to non-flying aspects of all pilot training. The aviator had an opportunity to set an example for the Afghan women, she said, who were training to fly fixed-wing aircraft. Clark hopes the impact made by the mission she made her own for a year went beyond producing capable pilots for the Afghan air force. "We exposed one culture to another and did our best to create an avenue for advancement in their society," she said.

Students trained by the 58th Special Operations Wing are turned into combat-ready special operations and rescue crew members who can make an impact in operations around the world. Due to cultural restrictions on interaction between men and women outside the family environment, it helped the Afghan women to have a female instructor, Clark said. The women were not invited to evening study sessions male students would hold, and were somewhat on their own when coalition instructors were not holding a formal class. Clark was able to provide an avenue for them to get questions answered and facilitate their self-study. "If they had a question they would come to me," Clark said. "They felt more comfortable having a woman present during training."

Clark helped the women to adapt to the training environment and served as a role model for them. "The women were all very motivated and competent. Despite facing significant threats to their safety, they did well in their training," she said. "These women were very brave to choose this career path. I was happy to be able to be an example of professionalism for them. I think it was important for them to see that a woman could become a pilot."

In addition to adjusting to the culture, Clark had to adjust to a different aircraft. To prepare for the mission, she had to learn how to fly the Mi-17, which is very different from the UH-1N. Because the Mi-17 rotor spins in the opposite direction, it has a different flight control arrangement, and it is much larger than the Huey. "I got 35 hours in the Mi-17 before I deployed," Clark said. "And the transition was smooth. It was fun." Once Clark had established herself as a well-trained and skilled pilot, she gained credibility with male and female students alike.

The major also had to deal with not only the dangers inherent to the deployed environment, but the heightened alert following a spate of inside attacks from Taliban members. "It's terrorists targeting their own people," she said. "You had to be on guard, but you can't be paranoid. A year is just too long to be paranoid." More traditional combat-related threats called Clark into action. She took part in a rescue mission after a helicopter was struck from an improvised explosive device during a training mission, and some of her Afghan comrades were killed in the line of duty. This included a safety officer she had advised throughout her year there who was killed in a grenade attack a week before she left the country.

The female Afghan pilots Clark worked with also had to deal with constant dangers. While on base, the women were protected, but they could not wear their uniforms in public without making themselves a target of the Taliban, Clark said. A competent air force to defend gains Afghanistan has made toward a free society will also translate into a more enlightened society in the long term, she said. "You have to change an entire generation," Clark said. "Our presence as advisers, Airmen, and, in my case, as a woman, served to enlighten the younger generation of Afghan soldiers we interacted with. This willingness to embrace a global perspective, coupled with the establishment of national pride, is essential for the country to defeat terrorist threats to their government and way of life."

"I encountered many intelligent and motivated Afghans," she continued. "With coalition support we saw many successes, such as Afghan officers becoming instructor pilots and leading real-world missions as well as taking command and leading their own people. As NATO troops withdraw over the next year it will be incumbent on these leaders to continue these practices as they assume primary responsibility for defending their country and their freedom."

> At the end of the battle, leave a country and their next generation enlightened.

～

"Every officer is a teacher." —L. A. Pennington

Adapted from "Female Aviator Makes Difference Training Afghan AF," by Jim Fisher, 377th Air Base Wing Public Affairs, December 26, 2014.

~

Life Lesson #29

It Was a Way of Life

During the Cold War, Arnie Sisk was directly involved with weapon systems that could launch nuclear missiles. Collectively, the USS *Ethan Allen* had more fire power than all armament used in World War II, including those dropped on Hiroshima and Nagasaki.

A native of Los Angeles, Sisk came from good stock. He was a fusion of hardworking farmers from Minnesota and Jewish immigrants from Russia seeking a better life in the United States. With only a small amount of formal education, but with tremendous ability, the agricultural side of his lineage could fix anything mechanical. Simply put, Arnie Sisk had an amazing, diverse group of relatives.

The year was 1964. Based on his academic accomplishments, Sisk was accepted into the prestigious U.S. Naval Academy. A mere seventeen years of age, he was too young for the draft, yet was proactively signing up to serve our country in the navy. Venturing east to Annapolis, Sisk's life would be changed forever as his personal core values were enhanced.

Armed with academic skills, tenacity, and strong work ethic, the academy enhanced Sisk's core values with self-dependence, teamwork, code of honor, physical fitness, and the importance of building personal relationships. Strengthened by these valuable core strengths, Sisk became a "whole man." With that foundational work ethic, traceable to his parents, he embraced the academic disciplines required of the academy and flourished.

Never an athlete, Sisk was thrust into playing sports. Learning to take care of yourself physically was embedded in each midshipman. When you are young, it tends to be a macho thing, but as you age, this value is critical to a happy and healthy life. Exercise is a natural part of the Naval Academy rigors.

In his senior year, Sisk took the road less traveled in academics, taking elective advanced courses in mathematics and physics. He eventually became a National Science Foundation Fellow after graduation. Recognizing his academic accomplishments, the navy offered Sisk the opportunity to graduate immediately into the master's program in computer science at Stanford as an officer.

Sisk qualified to work on nuclear submarines as an engineer. After rigorous training in nuclear power generation, he reported to his first assignment in 1971 aboard the USS *Guardfish* a nuclear powered attack submarine. Lieutenant Sisk served on deployment for six months in the western Pacific. One of the assignments on his second ship, the USS *Ethan Allen* (nuclear powered ballistic missile submarine), directly involved verifying the validity of release orders for the missiles. According to Sisk, "the feature film, *Crimson Tide,* accurately depicted the interaction between CO Gene Hackman and XO Denzel Washington regarding weapons release orders."

"Just like in the movie, you go on a submarine patrol and everyone's life is dependent on each other. It's not lip service; survival absolutely depends on being a team player. The consequence of bad performance was much more significant than most civilians' tasks."

"Living on a big machine" is submarine life as described by Sisk. "Personal relationships matter. As a strategic deterrent, you grow to be dependent on each other like a big fraternity." Completing his military service in 1982, his experiences would stay with him the rest of his life, especially the core value of interdependence. For Arnie Sisk, his military service was much more than a job; it was a way of life.

Facing a different kind of war, uterine cancer had struck his wife, Candi. Her courage and bravery over the course of a three year, personal war gave the couple an opportunity to talk about life and life's choices. At a support group called weSPARK, Sisk and his wife heard a core value that resonated. *Live in the moment and be present.* Not an overly religious guy, Sisk believes that it's the people in your life that really matter and how you embrace those relationships. Sadly, Candi, best friend and spouse for twenty-eight years, passed away in July 2010. Faced with his biggest choice ever, Sisk pressed ahead with life, choosing to lean on friendships for support.

Arnie Sisk's tenacity and determination came from layers of experience traced back to a life transformed by military service. "Not self, but country" was a key element of that transformation.

> At the end of the battle, time in the service was never just a job, it was a way of life . . . preparing us for the rest of our life's journey.

~

"The art of life is to know how to enjoy a little and to endure very much." —William Hazlitt

~

Life Lesson #30

Lean In

Today's soldiers have a great challenge. We are a nation with 19 million Veterans, but the vast majority of Americans have never worn a uniform or taken an oath to defend our freedom. That also includes our elected government officials. There's a very good chance that the civilian world misunderstands Veterans.

Knowing that there will be a beginning and an end to your military service, the importance of a supportive family buoyed by a strong faith will provide a "constancy" through the seasons of military service. As our soldiers return to the communities that they loved, who will support them as they pursue "doing what they say they value"?

Pete Moore had a supporting family going into and exiting his military career. He entered the army as private first class. Some thirty years later, three wars and six engagements, he departed as a lieutenant colonel having led five thousand soldiers. Growing up in Memphis, Moore was backed by a family and friends who had purpose. His dad was a building contractor and his mom, a nurse, raised three sons. The Moore family core values of helping others and standing up for what is right were their cornerstones.

The Moores were a patriotic bunch steeped in military service. Pete's dad served in the Korean War; his godfather and numerous cousins also fought in Vietnam. Sadly, his godfather perished in

Southeast Asia. This loss made him question whether he should serve his country, but his patriotism never wavered. Freedom for all, equality for all, and the right to pursue happiness really meant something to the Moores.

Pete always leaned deeply into his community and that included public school teachers like Helen. "She was a neighborhood family friend and public school teacher in the toughest parts of Memphis, and taught me the values of using my God-given talents for a greater purpose. In this tough city, you learned the value of fighting those who bullied their way through life." Under his dad's employment, Pete developed a strong work ethic. As the youngest of three sons, he always wanted to prove himself. He would lift the heaviest objects at a construction site and climb the tallest scaffolding where others were afraid to go. He simply liked those challenges and met them head on.

A bit adventurous, Pete became a strong, competitive swimmer and eventually a lifeguard. At only fourteen years of age, this strapping six foot two, 185 pound kid used his skills to save the lives of a thirty-two-year-old father and his son. Acting quickly can save lives. At age twenty-two, the desire to help others and the quest for adventure propelled Pete into the military. Entering the army a little bit older than most, in strong, physical shape, he completed boot camp at Ft. Leonard Wood, Missouri (also known as Ft. Lost in the Woods), in seemingly easy fashion. Memphis had prepared him.

Pete spent his military career in units that were organized for first deployment. Engaging in Desert Storm, Operation Desert Shield, Operation Enduring Freedom, and Iraqi Freedom, Pete's units were "first to serve" in a total of nine conflicts. With maximum flexibility, his troops could be ready to deploy within eighteen hours. Well trained in his assigned tasks, he often had legions of soldiers ready and buttoned up. To this day, he is able to figure things out rapidly. He spent a lot of time doing dangerous missions. Many a man were killed or injured. Pete would ask "why me? Why was I always spared? God's hand must have been on me."

Having moved twenty-two times over the course of his military career, often while he was deployed, Pete credits his wife for managing the war at home. Her flexibility and tenacity in redeploying their three boys and all of life's possessions from base to base was meritorious service beyond the call of duty.

For a soldier used to jumping out of plane, ready for deployment within hours, and leading a joint taskforce of thousands, he sensed a great advantage. Pete knew what God's promise was for him. If he died in battle, he knew where he was going. Buoyed by a strong, faith-filled wife, he could rest knowing that life was okay and going well at home. Pete's deep trust and faith freed him to go lead soldiers and complete their mission.

> At the end of the battle, knowing that change is constant, lean into your foundation of friends and faith.

Navy Lieutenant Shields Wilson nearly drowned during training and survived a torpedo attack en route to England. "I was connected with something bigger and that meant God." —Shields Wilson

⟿

"The constants in life are faith and family."

~

Life Lesson #31

Dealing with Guilt

Some Vietnam Veterans struggle with forgiving the government for using and betraying them. Other Veterans might have to forgive the American public for ignoring or scorning them. Soldiers may have to forgive the world for being unfair and for being cruel.

If self-forgiveness seems like a lot to expect from yourself, it is; but it's also essential. To withhold forgiveness means to cut yourself off from a compelling force deep in the soul that seeks it. If that forgiving force is denied, vitality and peace remain elusive. If you have been unable to achieve forgiveness, you might arrive at the end of your life filled with bitterness. Stockpiling transgressions of others (blame) or self (guilt) is the recipe for creating bitterness. Bitterness is a poison that contaminates even the most innocent heart. It is not too late to make a different decision. If you find yourself bitter, you can decide to learn how to forgive your transgression or your transgressor.

Wanting to forgive is an essential, often forgotten, element of for-giveness. Affirmation or prayer can help achieve this: *"Dear God: Help me want to forgive myself for _____,"* or simply say in the mirror *"I want to forgive _____* (myself, person, situation)" until you mean it. Then, you'll be ready to do the work. This kind of readiness is important, and readiness takes some cultivation. Be patient with yourself and respect whether or not you are ready to forgive.

False forgiveness serves no one and can be counterproductive. For example, telling yourself: *"I let that go a long time ago"* or *"It's over and forgotten,"* can become an excuse for not doing the work of forgiveness. If you are unable, unwilling, or not yet ready to forgive, patiently wait for another opportunity and reconsider it later. As health issues force external changes upon you, internal changes will also ensue. These changes are often good, fostering growth and opportunity.

If you suffer from unmourned grief from fallen comrades or unforgiven guilt from acts you did or failed to do during military service, you might want to consider creating a ceremony to lay these burdens down; you've carried them long enough.

> At the end of the battle, unforgiven guilt can sabotage your life and undermine peaceful dying.

∼

"Open up to the possibility of forgiveness." —Deborah Grassman, www.opuspeace.org

~

Life Lesson #32

Speed Up the Epiphany

Caring for Veterans is important to Michael Kaplan. He has been driven by his own experience and self-discovery.

Serving our nation from 1982 to 1987 in the Active Guard and Reserve, combined with two other careers, Kaplan never knew a gap from military service. His life was always connected to Veterans. "Dare say, I was being led. I simply love watching Veterans become successful."

Managing a Veterans service organization, Phase II Advantage, Kaplan seeks to understand Veterans' barriers to success. He has found that Veterans don't believe in the American dream any more. Further, they generally think that the landscape of corporations, under their current political platform, would not provide opportunities to them. With that premise, Kaplan focused on fixing the people piece and not attacking a system issue. On a new quest to show Veterans where they were the strongest, Michael Kaplan burrowed into how Veterans were wired, understood their mindset, and focused on applying their strengths. "You lay it out for our Veterans and make them believe in themselves."

Veterans have to learn how to transition from one life to another. They must acknowledge their true value and how job skills can be applied. If a sniper coming out of the service does not think his skills are relevant to the restaurant world, he's wrong. Veterans simply underestimate the amount of value they can bring to the table. Consider what a Veteran has experienced in basic training:

- *Deconstruction* that strips down the soldier, removing anything negative.
- *Replacement and reassemble*, creating an aggregate team that is stronger.
- *Training* to face all extremities.
- *Send them forward* mission ready.

Kaplan uses the same process to bring Veterans into civilian life. He takes them through deconstruction, replacement, retraining/upgrading, and redeployment to get over entrenched lies and myths about corporate America. One example is Brian, who came to Kaplan saying that he did not have the business sense to make it. "I can never be a success with my background, pedigree or education!"

"Excuses are entrenched," according to Kaplan. Reflecting on his own past, when Kaplan built his first restaurant, he had zero experience in the industry. Without a clue of how to operate a restaurant, he quickly learned on the job, mirroring his military journey. Working on a shoestring budget for three years, he learned, persevered, applied his skills, and eventually sold his first restaurant that was doing $1.5 million in sales. Clueless, yet armed with a military drive and attention to detail, Michael credits his baseline experience from the army. This happens every day with Veterans who work with Kaplan.

Brian thought that he did not have any ability to sell and certainly feared meeting with the chief executive officer (CEO) at a company. Coming from the Infantry and Combat Arms, Brian had been trained in 360 degree awareness. Walking into the CEO's office, he quickly spotted a class ring in the office, a familiar-looking diploma, and a lapel pin on the executive's jacket. Seeing incredible detail as if he is out in the field looking for IEDs (improvised explosive devices), Brian had an authentic conversation that sounded like he had known this executive for twenty years.

They walked out and Kaplan commented: "You don't think you can sell, but you just signed a contract with a C-suite." He pointed out Brian's skill set and Brian now consciously uses his military training as a foundation to his personal success. Describing Brian as a "world-class mentalist," Kaplan has observed him walking into an office, sizing up the surroundings, and establishing an instant bond.

You can overcome the preconceived barriers that you aren't capable of succeeding in the civilian world. Michael Kaplan creates an environment and rewired mindset where Veterans can speed up their own personal epiphany, understand their true skills, and identify their new purpose in life. The light bulb will go on at the right time for all the right reasons for an individual who is ready to land and go forward.

Kaplan's own epiphany occurred nine years after he officially left the military. While on an international fugitive squad for the FBI in Central and South America and then high-threat executive protection, he met corporate leaders who debunked his own myths about the rich. They weren't born with a silver spoon in their mouths nor expected a free ride. They were hardworking, Horatio Alger types that were just like regular Joes.

At the end of the battle, speed up your epiphany by getting a mentor who can be a life and business coach, just like a battle buddy.

"We often have to deconstruct our own self barriers to channel true strengths." —Michael Kaplan

~

Life Lesson #33

Duty and Honor Return Home to Sherman, Texas

In 2015, Cecil Douglas returned to his hometown of Sherman, Texas, after dedicating thirty-eight years to the military and (in supporting positions) to our U.S. government. In our cities, and in our country, Veterans like Douglas are needed for their experience, intellect, and character to build stronger communities.

Growing up in Sherman, sixty miles north of Dallas, Douglas was taught by his faith-filled mom to always look out for others. When he joined the military in 1975, that core value was strengthened one hundred fold.

Basic training in Fort Ord, California, was tough. Motivated to be the best, Douglas was torn down to be built up again. Taught to keep himself alive and protect his buddies, he was led by a very strict Drill Sergeant Thomas. Focused on making his unit a disciplined unit of interdependent soldiers, the Houston native drill sergeant made it tougher on the Texas native Douglas. "Son, as a Texan, we are tougher and we don't let people run over us."

Put to the test in conditions "worse than two-a-day football practices in humid, hot August," an additional challenge came from carrying a weapon everywhere and running constantly. "As a team, we got into the very best physical shape of our lives, were trained to fight and survive, and picked up basic skills in marching, as well as drilling ceremonies. Nearing the end of basic, the ole Sarge turned out to be a very good person. We might have gone in as a team, but we came out one strong unit of soldiers."

Over the course of the next several decades, Douglas served in Fort Carson, Colorado. He was deployed to Third Infantry, Kitzingen, Germany, in 1981. Finding out what the real army was like through the infantry division, the 248 soldiers trained 230 days in the field each year preparing for war.

In 1985, stationed in Pirmasen, Germany, Supply Sergeant Douglas served in 59th Ordinance Brigade reporting to General Bradford. Taking care of the junior brigade underneath them—1,500 soldiers—the units were constantly inspected. When the general arrived, he picked apart the 59th ordinance and the standards changed. Weaknesses were identified and Douglas's team inspected junior brigades with new expectations "plusing themselves up."

With new, higher expectations, Douglas believed that "if I expected a man to be perfect, I needed to be perfect myself." Transformed by working for this general, Douglas described any tasks accomplished under Bradford as done "carefully, taking time to analyze the situation, determine what a team needs to do to accomplish a mission, come up with a bulletproof plan and execute the plan. The things I know now, I wish I would have known back then. Hindsight is truly 20/20."

Eventually Douglas landed at the DCA (Director of Community Activity), succeeding as a logistics manager and rising seven levels from GS 4 to GS 11. With the conviction that he would be the military's very best supply professional, Douglas always strived to better himself.

The DCA leadership trusted and believed in him knowing that he had the knowledge to make the army go. Effectively training young soldiers, Douglas's team made sure that platoons were equipped and ready for combat with the right vehicles, armory, ammunition, and resources to accomplish their mission. He led with pride, dedication, and discipline—core values that will reach back to the next generation of Sherman, Texas, and beyond.

As Douglas returns to his original Texas hometown, his message to teenagers in Sherman is this: Finish school, get a job, or join the armed forces. Most importantly, be the change you wish to see in the world today.

At the end of the battle, carry your core values of protecting one another back to build stronger communities.

"Veterans can rebuild purpose at home not only by finding the strength within themselves, but by helping others—through community service and volunteering." —www.GotYour6.org

~

Life Lesson #34

Twelve Layers of Manhood

There are few soldiers who fought in World War II, the Korean War, and the Vietnam War. But one did, and at the center were twelve core principles for personal conduct that guided him and his troops through combat.

The son of a janitor and a hardworking mother in suburban Philadelphia, Julius Becton entered a segregated U.S. Army at age eighteen. During his forty-year career, he served in all three wars and eventually rose to the rank of lieutenant general. Battling through a number of harrowing situations as part of an all-black battalion, he was wounded by shrapnel in a firefight in Korea. Deployed to Vietnam in 1967, he was the commander of the Cavalry Squadron in the 101st Airborne. Among his decorations are the Distinguished Service Medal, two Silver Stars, two Legion of Merit medals, and two Purple Hearts.

Following retirement, Becton joined the Reagan administration in 1984 as director of the Office of Foreign Assistance for the Agency for International Development. From 1985 to 1989, he was director of the Federal Emergency Management Agency (FEMA). His final civilian post was as superintendent of public schools in the District of Columbia. He has been listed many times by *Ebony* magazine as "One of the 100 Most Influential Blacks in America."

Core Principles for Personal Conduct

1. Be professional.
2. Integrity is nonnegotiable.
3. Loyalty is a two-way street.
4. Follow the chain of command.
5. Innovate and seek a better way.
6. Disagreement is not disrespect.
7. Admit mistakes.
8. Challenge assertions.
9. Never abuse or misuse people.
10. Security and safety are everyone's business.
11. Maintain your sense of humor.
12. Keep things in perspective.

At the end of the battle, center your life on core principles.

∼

"Stay true to the guiding philosophy of integrity above all."
—Lieutenant General Julius Wesley Becton Jr.

~

Life Lesson #35

Bridging the Gap of Misunderstanding

"Military service fundamentally changed my life." Working in politics on Capitol Hill, Commander Mark S. Kirk realized that he couldn't effectively advise on military matters without personal experience, so he volunteered for a direct commission in the navy.

Today's battlefield is a separate realm. The distance between stateside and "boots on the ground" is vast. As Rebecca Frankel stated in *War Dogs*, "when we cannot make the human connection over war, we cannot empathize or imagine the far off world of a combat zone. . . . Those military working dogs are a bridge over the divide."

When the country fought its previous wars, it was family first with fathers and sons in harm's way with mothers and daughters working in defense plants. For two decades after World War II, the standing force remained so large that most Americans had a direct military connection. Among older baby boomers, those born before 1955, at least three-quarters have had an immediate family member—sibling, parent, spouse, child—who served in uniform. Of Americans born since 1980, one in three millennials are closely related to someone with military experience.

Deciding he needed personal experience, Kirk served in the Office of Naval Intelligence, was detailed to the Central Intelligence Agency, and then served as a watch officer for the Navy Desk at the Pentagon.

He went on to fly as an air crewman on the Prowler aircraft. For Kirk, there is no substitute for realizing the inherent dangers if you aren't close enough to the action. You can't question our military strategy or competence without familiarity.

> At the end of the battle, we must close the distance gap in understanding military in order to govern properly.

～

"Most Americans were familiar enough with the military to respect it while being sharply aware of its shortcomings, as they were with the school system, their religion, and other important and fallible institutions."

"When you wear the uniform, it changes you." —Mark S. Kirk, Commander, Navy, Kosovo and Afghan conflicts

"Pop culture television and film will not close the gap between warriors and civilians."

~

Life Lesson #36

Looking for the Legacy

Many Vietnam Veterans prefer that their legacy be remembered in a positive light. Bob Stockhausen's voice may represent many Vietnam Veterans' views: "Our generation was the one that figured out you can oppose the war, but support the troops," he said. "Even though our welcome home was 15 years late, we're out on the front line welcoming home the troops from Iraq and Afghanistan."

Some Vietnam Vets believe that their legacy from the lessons of the Vietnam War have yet to be learned. Mary Reynolds Powell, 62, of Cleveland, is still proud of her experience as an army nurse in Vietnam. "I am the person I am today because I went through it," she said. But Powell believes the United States still hasn't learned how to fight a war while considering the potential political, social, cultural, and historic ramifications, an oversight ultimately dooming any military action overseas. "We championed the PTSD issue, the Agent Orange issue and the POW/MIA issue," Stockhausen said. "You *can* change things. But you have to be willing to work at it."

On a very personal level, the Vietnam War experience made stronger people, a more caring community, and opened up America's eyes to the horrors of war. It's not all Hollywood crap. It's a very scary, horrible place to be.

At the end of the battle, something positive comes from every war and conflict.

"Thank you to the Vietnam Veterans and their families for the sacrifices that they made. They have taught us that no matter what our positions may be on policy, as Americans and patriots, we must support our troops with our thoughts and prayers." —Zach Wamp

~

Life Lesson #37

Sliver of Humanity

Originally from San Francisco, Todd Dudley bucked much of the "left coast" liberal mindset. His youth was shaped by service as an Eagle Scout and sharpened by the disciplines required as a competitive swimmer. Setting his sights early for a structured life, he applied and was accepted to the Naval Academy. In 1993, he became a navy pilot and devoted the next twenty-one years to serving our country.

Dudley's military service during the Balkan conflict, and later in Afghanistan, dramatically opened his eyes to the human condition in war-torn societies. The daily grind of poverty, and pervasive sense of hopelessness, sapped the joy of living from the entire landscape. It gave military service members an extraordinary appreciation for what is right in America. "Serving America overseas is always a watershed moment. When you are sent on a mission to restore order in a country, your perspective of your own country is changed forever."

For example, during his 2011 deployment to Kabul, Afghanistan, Dudley witnessed a country where the rule of law was still largely in tatters. Reflecting on the human conditions he witnessed in Kabul, violence transformed the face of the city. "Under adverse conditions where rule of law is lacking, it became quickly apparent what humans are capable of doing to each other. This violence altered Kabul into a city characterized by 20' blast walls, police and private security forces, and innumerable security checkpoints. Kabul became a city of constant violence and hopelessness.

Dudley recalls that "building and barriers are one thing, but witnessing actual human suffering is quite another. Ensconced behind barriers, his team got a humanitarian call to support a relief mission to Badam Bagh, a women's prison located near Kabul. Dudley called his wife, located back at their home in Germany at the time, asking her to rally their daughter's Girl Scout troop to gather boxes of clothing and toys as a charitable donation to the women prisoners.

American troops witnessed women who had gone through physical and emotional abuse. It was widely believed that many of these women had been imprisoned for the act of fleeing their abusive husbands, and were thrown behind bars with their children to rot away. "American soldiers see the world's most depraved conditions. They don't deploy to exotic places like the south of France, on African safaris, or vacation spots at Caribbean beach resorts. American troops are deployed to some of the most difficult places on earth, from parts of Africa ravaged by Ebola, or the most remote villages of Afghanistan. Our troops are there, doing the hard work, every day."

Dudley consequently developed a special empathy for the neediest children of Kabul. "Children were thrust in the middle of all this hate and violence. When on patrol, we would always be flocked by little children." Todd made it a point to distribute various pens, pencils, and candy to the least fortunate of these, usually the little girls who were always pushed to the back of the line.

"War-torn Afghanistan gives very little hope for these little girls. Boisterous boys will always be boisterous boys, but it was very clear in Todd's mind that opportunities afforded to the young girls in this society were very limited, and often got worse as they got older. Offering gifts to the little girls, in the very back of the throng of kids, was therefore something special. Todd would always ask the boys if he might give the gifts to the young lady hiding in the back of the group, and let her distribute the candies. The girls' eyes would light right up! In daily life, few people had ever spoken to the "least of these" with compassion. No one ever gave them the time of day, much less an opportunity to feel a sense of pride, or to feel valued. All he could do was to show them a little sliver of humanity. Such experiences made an indelible mark on Todd Dudley.

At the end of the battle, a soldier's perspective can be leveraged to build America back.

"Because Veterans have a different perspective, they are better prepared to influence the building of communities here in America. They have a galvanized spirit and set of skills that can create change . . . especially from the life lessons they learned. Americans may never understand the cruelty, the crushing poverty and injustice so evident in third world countries." —Todd Dudley

~

Life Lesson #38

Getting a Leg Up

Lessons were many for Captain Gordon Logan (Air Force 1969–1976), but teamwork tops the list. "You interact with people from all walks of life, but are brought together to complete a mission and that accomplishment requires interdependence." As an aircraft commander of a Hercules C-130, Logan learned first to take care of his team. "When you take care of your people, they will take care of you. You must consider everyone on the team as important and that your team is only as strong as its weakest link. Working together, you can accomplish a heck of a lot more than working as individuals."

The C-130 Hercules, capable of operating from rough, dirt airstrips, is a prime transport for para-dropping troops and cargo into hostile areas. Originally built in 1954 by Lockheed, over 2,400 have been constructed and over half are still in service today. Teamwork began by having discipline, building competencies and strong skills, and following the system. The C-130 carried a pilot, co-pilot, navigator, flight engineer, load master, and mechanic who deeply understood the plane. All played important, interdependent roles.

The load master was responsible for proper loading of cargo and weight distribution aboard the C-130. When the crew did a low altitude parachute extraction system (LAPES), flying ten feet off the ground to drop a 2,200-pound cargo load with a parachute attached, your team had to make sure it was perfectly rigged, managing the exact center of gravity. There was no margin for error. Team precision was also paramount when parachutes pull a 42,000-pound load from the aircraft. When the load is clear of the plane, parachutes inflate and lower the load to the ground.

Flying into remote parts of the world, including the varied terrain of Southeast Asia, the flight engineer had to be quick enough to work around issues. The navigator had to get the plane to the targeted spot or airfield. If the navigator failed, his mistakes would be costly.

Fortunately, Logan's C-130 crew avoided any hair-raising missions and won't be highlighted in a Clint Eastwood feature film. Logan has experienced that great teamwork in the military creates a bridge over to civilian life. Within his company, SportClips, over fifty Veterans are thriving as franchisees because they moved their organizational and teamwork skills to Logan's outfit.

Most importantly, Logan and the International Franchise System has generated over 150,000 jobs for Veterans and their spouses creating the "next logical career step." Uniquely suited to franchise operations, Veterans are succeeding as members of process-oriented teams. They understand the importance of executing within a system, are responsive to codependency, and responsible for achieving a mission. Logan notes, "The military has done a very good job of teaching these valuable life skills and creating disciplines."

"The focus and understanding of how all the pieces work together toward accomplishing mission is deeply entrenched in Veterans. It's second nature after having gone through military training. Similarly, SportClips is very structured, complete with precise check lists. Our DNA mirrors a mission oriented outfit from any branch of the military." A natural by-product of piloting a C-130, Logan stated that nothing is left to chance as SportClips works off an extensive check list—just like his flight crew. All details, big and small, are thoroughly documented. They are understandable, readable, and translatable into action, proving to be a very effective process for SportClips.

According to Logan, franchises go through plenty of their own LAPES today. Logan cited that the "strong leadership skills coming from an NCO or Squadron Leader, directs a team through their own harrowing business situations. Core values such as setting an example, not asking people to do things that you aren't willing to do, and walking the talk (from the Vietnam era), are fundamental to business success.

At the end of the battle, life lessons learned in the military give Veterans a leg up to be a business success.

"Veterans may have to shore up on how to run a business, but the core skills are in place to be successful, starting with teamwork and leading to accomplish a mission." —Gordon Logan, CEO and founder, SportClips

~

Life Lesson #39

Jacob's Ladder

Jacob Younginer served nobly in the United States Air Force from 1964 to 1992. His "Jacob's Ladder" has eleven rungs of lessons. Climb to the top for a Veteran's view.

1. Seize every opportunity.
2. Don't wait for the opportunity to come along to prepare for it, but be prepared for any opportunity that comes along.
3. Don't expect special favors. Go out and earn that opportunity.
4. Be prepared.
5. Always commit yourself to doing the better job than everybody else first.
6. Always do it in a pleasant attitude.
7. Always be fair to everybody. But do your job and be the person that they can depend on to do a wonderful job.
8. And build that as your reputation and your legacy.
9. Don't try to slough off and not carry your full share of the load.
10. But be the kind of person that they can depend on and that they will depend on.
11. Yes, you're going to get a lot of extra tasks and a lot of extra piled on you because you're doing that. And you're that kind of person.

And at the end of the battle, always be proud of what you do. Write your name on it with pride. If you do that, you will go far in life regardless of what career you choose.

~

Life Lesson #40

VE Day: Solemn Gratitude and Mixed Jubilation

Arthur Scattergood's memoir begins with an innocent family outing in the fall of 1939; when his father learns of the invasion of Poland, he points to fifteen-year-old Arthur to say, "This is the beginning of World War II. And you will serve in it." Four years later, Arthur was inducted into the air corps, but in the wake of D-Day he was reassigned to the infantry, which needed more troops. His unit, assigned to Patton's Third Army, drove hard toward Berlin, and then veered south toward Czechoslovakia, where they marked VE Day.

To Arthur, there was no way to describe the fear of a soldier, especially one on the front line like the infantry. Often, as their American forces advanced, the German resistance seemed to strengthen. One motivating factor was "just consider what the U.S. will look like if under the German flag."

Arthur set down his account of war as well as the lessons he learned from his experience fifty years after the war ended. Some of those memories he tried hard to forget.

Arthur Scattergood, Army, WWII, 1939–1945

At the end of the battle, the fear has subsided to solemn gratitude and mixed jubilation.

∼

"In war, there is no substitute for victory." —General Douglas MacArthur

~

Life Lesson #41

Still Playing Taps

Eight thousand three hundred and one American soldiers are buried about six miles from Maastricht, in the Netherlands. They lost their lives in the battle Operation Market Garden, fighting to liberate Holland in the fall and winter of 1944.

Every single soldier buried in the cemetery, as well as those in the Canadian and British military cemeteries, has been personally adopted by a Dutch family who minds the grave, decorates them, and upholds the tradition of gratefulness. The Dutch have also maintained the custom of keeping a portrait of "their" American soldier in a place of honor in their home.

Each year on Liberation Day, memorial services are held for "the men who died to liberate Holland." The day concludes with a concert. The final piece is always "Il Silenzio," a memorial piece commissioned by the Dutch and first played in 1965 on the 20th anniversary of Holland's liberation. It has been the concluding piece of the memorial concert ever since.

In 2014, the soloist was a thirteen-year-old Dutch girl, Melissa Venema, backed by André Rieu and the Royal Orchestra of the Netherlands. This beautiful concert piece is based upon the original version of taps and was composed by Italian composer Nino Rossi. Shed a tear by visiting www.flixxy.com/trumpet-solo-melissa-venema.htm.

Where Americans are buried across Europe defending their freedom.

1. American Cemetery in Aisne-Marne, France. A total of 2,289.
2. American Cemetery in Ardennes, Belgium. A total of 5,329.
3. American Cemetery in Brittany, France. A total of 4,410.
4. American Cemetery in Brookwood, England. A total of 468.
5. Cambridge, England. A total of 3,812.
6. American Cemetery in Epinal, France. A total of 5,525.
7. Flanders Field, Belgium. A total of 368.
8. Florence, Italy. A total of 4,402.
9. Henri-Chapelle, Belgium. A total of 7,992.
10. Lorraine, France. A total of 10,489.
11. Luxembourg, Luxembourg. A total of 5,076.
12. Meuse-Argonne. A total of 14,246.
13. Netherlands, Netherlands. A total of 8,301.
14. Normandy, France. A total of 9,387.
15. Oise-Aisne, France. A total of 6,012.
16. Rhone, France. A total of 861.
17. Sicily, Italy. A total of 7,861.
18. Somme, France. A total of 1,844.
19. St. Mihiel, France. A total of 4,153.
20. Suresnes, France. A total of 1,541.

The count is 104,366 brave Americans.

At the end of the battle, may the gratitude "play on" for our fallen Americans in Europe.

~

Epilogue

History Is in Your Hands

With the completion of this inaugural *Life Lessons from Veterans* book, you now have "history in your hands." With time marching on, your challenge is to record the war stories within your own family before they are lost to dementia or death.

That puts the writing of history in *your* hands.

Through countless conversations, the greatest lesson learned has been to stop and listen to stories both great and small. Every single Veteran's story has a touch of heroism, courage, bravery, and patriotism. The biggest regret is that we could not share all of them in this one book.

This we know: our country has heart and it beats through our Veterans. We, as a country, will never "go quietly." Fueled by the spirit of our Veterans, we will never be driven by fear, especially when it comes to the violation of the rights of others. This spirit has never burned brighter.

And at the end of the battle, our Veterans have served our country well and we are thankful . . . very thankful.

～

"Those who cannot remember the past are condemned to repeat it." —George Santayana

Text Credits

"Writing History," permission granted by www.davisenterprise.net, Anne Ternus-Bellamy, "Learning the Lessons of War from Those Who Fought," January 7, 2014; additional permission granted by Veterans History Project, Library of Congress, 2015.

"Our Squadron Janitor," permission granted by Colonel James Moschgat, Retired.

"The School Desks," permission granted by David Sargent, creekwoodcc.org, 2015.

"Veteran's Day Poem," permission granted by Roger Hancock, 2015.

"Size of the Heart," permission granted by University of Texas, Office of External Affairs.

"You Had the Rice Seeds," permission granted by Texas A&M University Press, 2015.

"Code Talker," permission granted by Texas Military Forces Museum, Camp Mabry, Austin, Texas.

"Wings Across America," permission granted by Wings Across America, 2015.

"Far Better to Dare Mighty Things," permission granted by Veterans History Project and Library of Congress; additional permission requested to We Are the Mighty, 2015.

"Semper Fi Leadership," permission granted by Jeff Clement, © 2015 *The Lieutenant Don't Know*.